THE CUSTER ALBUM

"In this country, no man, particularly if moderately educated, need fail in life if determined to succeed, so many and varied are the avenues to honorable employment which open on all hands before him."

GEORGE ARMSTRONG CUSTER

the CUSTER ALBUM

A PICTORIAL BIOGRAPHY OF GENERAL GEORGE A. CUSTER

By Lawrence A. Frost

BONANZA BOOKS
NEW YORK

Copyright © MCMLXIV by Superior Publishing Company, Seattle, Washington

This 1984 edition is published by Bonanza Books, distributed by Crown Publishers, Inc. by arrangement with the author.

Manufactured in the United States of America

Library of Congress Cataloging in Publication Data

Frost, Lawrence A.
 The Custer album.

 Originally published: Seattle : Superior Pub. Co., 1964.
 Bibliography: p.
 Includes index.
 1. Custer, George Armstrong, 1839–1876—Iconography.
2. Generals—United States—Iconography.   I. Title.
E467.1.C99F737   1984   973.8′2′0924 [B]   83-22309

ISBN: 0-517-427141

h g f e d c b

Dedication

Dedicated to Evelyn Luce and her husband, the late Major Edward S. Luce, 16 years superintendent of the Custer Battlefield National Monument.

CONTENTS

Author's Preface

It is my fate to live in a town steeped with Custer lore. The first house I lived in was across the street from members of the Custer family. They were the first people I became acquainted with there. When they left town just before World War II, their going-away gift to me was a pair of General Custer's cavalry boots.

One hardly can cross the city of Monroe without passing the equestrian statue of the General, or cross the River Raisin he once fished in.

The church that I attend is the one in which the General and Libbie Bacon were married.

Several years ago I hired an assistant who, weeks later, I discovered was living in General Custer's old home. Excellent assistant that she was, I have been accused of choosing her because of that fact.

Like the hometown of most people of note, one finds few people who laud him, or have any great amount of accurate information about him.

Over the years there have been innumerable attempts to deify or villify him. This variance of opinion began before his death and influences opinions to this very day. Few are they who can prove impartiality where Custer is concerned, though many claim it.

Any man whose abilities were so outstanding as to receive promotion upon promotion, notwithstanding the fact that the seniority rule prevailed in the army of the Civil War period, was bound to leave a bad taste in the mouths of the less able officers over whom he had leapt.

The North was given new hope when Custer's cavalry victories made the headlines, for up to that point Union cavalry victories were a rarity. It was natural that he became the *beau ideal* of cavalry. Generals who *led* men were rare; generals who *won* battles were rarer. It is no wonder that he was idolized from President Lincoln down. All the world loves a winner.

General Custer was a man of initiative and action. Quick thinking and quick acting, his chief concern was for the ultimate objective. Frequently this lead him to overlook the immediate comforts of those under him.

His critics said he was rash because his decisions were quick and decisive. The cavalry was no place for slow thinking, lethargic officers. Like the air force of today it was a mobil, flexible arm, ever alert and quick to act. In combat there is a time to strike which, if acted upon instantaneously, can be the factor deciding victory.

Many wonder why I bother to study the life of a soldier when there is so much material available about statesmen like Lincoln. I have but one answer. Lincoln didn't live here.

CUSTER'S LAST CHARGE
Custer's Todes=Ritt.

CUSTER'S LAST CHARGE. Over one hundred artists have attempted to portray what no white man lived to describe. This lithograph by Feodor Fuchs in 1876 is, perhaps, the earliest endeavor.

GENERAL CUSTER'S DEATH STRUGGLE. By H. Steinegger in 1878. Courtesy of the Library of Congress.

CUSTER'S LAST RALLY. In 1881, John Mulvany painted a canvas 20 × 11 feet, which was exhibited around the country. It, like many others, makes the error of exhibiting Custer with a sabre, a weapon that each man was ordered to leave behind. Courtesy of the Library of Congress.

CUSTER'S LAST CHARGE. By John A. Elder in 1884. Courtesy of the Library of Congress.

BATTLE OF THE BIG HORN. Custer is firing two revolvers at once, wearing a dress uniform, carrying a sabre, and wearing a dark hat on long hair. These are typical inaccuracies in most artists' conception of this famous battle. Even the terrain is unreal. This by Kurz and Allison was released in 1889. Courtesy of the Library of Congress.

CUSTER'S LAST FIGHT. Perhaps the goriest of all such pictures. This canvas was painted by Cassily Adams about 1888 and sold later to Anheuser-Busch, Inc. Mr. Busch gave it to the Seventh Cavalry, remaining in its hands until June 13, 1946, when it was destroyed by fire at Fort Bliss. Courtesy of the Library of Congress.

CUSTER'S LAST FIGHT. The most widely known painting depicting this western battle. By Otto Becker in 1895. Photo courtesy Anheuser-Busch, Inc.

Controversy enters into almost every discussion of any artist's interpretation of the Battle of the Little Big Horn. Though frequently shown otherwise; General Custer's hair was short; neither he nor his men carried sabres; Custer wore a light grey broad brimmed, low crowned hat and a buckskin suit with a "frontier fringe," his brother Tom being in similar dress; none of the men or officers were in full dress uniforms; very few of the Indians wore war bonnets. Since there were no white survivors any reconstruction of the battle is fair game for all.

CUSTER'S LAST STAND. By Edgar S. Paxson in 1899. Following 20 years of research and interviews the artist painted for eight years to complete this six by ten foot canvas. Courtesy of William Edgar Paxson and the Whitney Gallery of Western Art, Cody, Wyo.

CUSTER'S LAST FIGHT. By William R. Leigh. From the original painting in Woolaroc Museum, Bartlesville, Oklahoma.

CUSTER'S LAST STAND. By Theodore B. Pitman in 1953. Courtesy of John S. du Mont.

GENERAL CUSTER'S LAST BATTLE. By Elk Eber. Details are fairly accurate. Courtesy of the Custer Battlefield National Monument.

CUSTER'S FIGHT. Indians frequently drew pictographs to show some happening in their lives that had left a vivid impression. Here the Cheyenne "White Bird" has drawn his version of a portion of the Custer fight. Courtesy of the Custer Battlefield Museum.

CUSTER'S LAST HOPE. Painted by J. K. Ralston, 1959. Owned by Mr. and Mrs. Don C. Foote, Billings, Montana. Upper right depicts Sgt. James Butler riding toward Reno Hill for relief.

AFTER THE BATTLE. Painted by J. K. Ralston, 1955. Owned by Mr. and Mrs. Don C. Foote, Billings, Montana. A vivid portrayal of the aftermath of the Custer Battle based on 39 authenticated incidents.

ORGANIZING THE DEFENSE FOR THE LAST STAND. J. K. Ralston artist.

Chapter One

HIS FAMILY CALLED HIM AUTIE

Ohio is a state of generals. It took a Civil War to make that evident. The results of that war might have been different had the North not had Generals Ulysses Simpson Grant, William Tecumseh Sherman, Philip Henry Sheridan, and George Armstrong Custer, for those Ohioans played a major part in the defeat of the South.

Take that fateful third day at Gettysburg when the "Boy General" Custer led his Michigan Cavalry Brigade in a headlong assault against General J. E. B. Stuart's famed cavalry. Had Stuart's seemingly invincible cavalrymen not been routed at that particular moment, they would have been free to attack the rear of the Union forces on Cemetery Ridge. The Union chance of stopping them at that point would have been zero and Pickett's charge could have been successful. On the shoulders of one man can rest the fate of a decisive battle and so it did on that day that determined the turning point of the war. Custer personally led that attack against Stuart and defeated him.

George Armstrong Custer was born in the peaceful little village of New Rumley, Ohio, on December 5, 1839. The clang of steel was early in his ears for his father, Emanuel Custer, was the village blacksmith.

Emanuel's grandfather fought in the Revolution as a member of the Philadelphia County Militia. The mother of this grandfather was Sara Martha Ball, a cousin of the mother of General Washington.

Like most of his neighbors, Emanuel was a member of the militia. Whenever he drilled, George Armstrong, or "Autie" as he called his small son, accompanied him wearing a small militia uniform. After the *New Rumley Invincibles* had completed their drill it was a common occurrence to have the four-year-old go through the Scott's manual of arms with his toy musket. It was around this time that his father heard him repeat the line one of his older brothers was committing to memory for school: "My voice is for war."

As a boy, and even as a young man, he was always full of fun. He enjoyed a practical joke even if it was on himself. All of his playmates mention his gentle disposition and even temper. Though he was very strong for his age and easily able to throw the other boys in a wrestling match he was never known to use his strength in bullying others.

The sturdy blond lad was the oldest of Emanuel's second marriage. Emanuel's wife, Matilda Viers, had died six years after their marriage leaving him with three children. His second wife,

17

MARIA WARD KIRKPATRICK CUSTER. Born in Burgettstown, Pennsylvania in 1807, the General's mother lost her first husband, Israel R. Kirkpatrick, a year after the death of the first Mrs. Custer. She too was left with three small children. Mrs. E. B. Custer collection. Courtesy of the Custer Battlefield Museum.

Maria Ward, at the age of 16 married Israel R. Kirkpatrick. Kirkpatrick died one year after the passing of Emanuel's first wife, leaving three children. One daughter, Lydia Ann, was to marry David Reed of Monroe, Michigan and eventually provide Autie with a second home there.

Emanuel married Maria Ward Kirkpatrick in 1836. Of this second marriage were born in or near New Rumley, Ohio:

1. George Armstrong Custer, December 5, 1839.
2. Nevin Johnson Custer, July 29, 1842.
3. Thomas Ward Custer, March 15, 1845.
4. Boston Custer, October 31, 1848.
5. Margaret Emma Custer, January 5, 1852.

Though Autie's interest in military affairs began at an early age, his interest in horses developed at the same time. His father divided his time between farming and blacksmithing. Since horses were predominant in both endeavors, the lad had ample opportunity to be around them. Being the oldest

EMANUEL H. CUSTER. Autie's father was born in Cryssoptown, Maryland, in 1806. Settling in New Rumley as a young blacksmith, he married Matilda Viers at the age of 22. Six years later she died leaving him with three children. Mrs. E. B. Custer collection. Courtesy of the Custer Battlefield Museum.

his father gave him the responsibility of many small tasks around the farm and the blacksmith shop. To these early chores can be attributed the development of his love of animals and his powerful body.

Mrs. Custer was a family-loving soul and somehow Autie was her favorite. Perhaps it was the intense love and thoughtfulness he always displayed toward her. She was of a sickly nature and, though the others were good children, Autie was the most comforting.

While living in the village of New Rumley the children went to the district school. In the early fifties the family moved out about two miles into Harrison County to live in a log cabin. The children attended the Creal School a mile and a half north of Scio.

About the time that Autie had reached the age of ten, his half-sister, Lydia, married David Reed of Monroe, Michigan. Monroe was a town of 3,500 population; equal parts French, English and German. It was a lonely period for her that could only be relieved by constantly seeing some members of her family. Since it was impractical to travel by horse and buggy the 200 odd miles to New Rumley, it was decided to send young Autie to live with her until she became adjusted and acquainted with her new surroundings. This adventure was quite acceptable to the youngster.

Monroe had had a remarkable experience in 1813, just 36 years earlier. The second oldest settlement in Southern Michigan, it had undergone a horrible Indian massacre during the time the British general, Proctor, had offered a bounty to the Indians for American scalps. On the dawn of January 22nd,

400 persons lay dead in the ashes of Monroe; 650 were injured or missing.

Autie heard much of this as there still were many survivors always willing to tell newcomers and eager youngsters of their experiences. After two years schooling in Monroe, Autie returned to New Rumley to assist his father on the farm. This must have had its drawbacks for Emanuel recognized the educational advantages in Michigan and sent Autie back to Monroe at the end of two years. A good father, he wanted his children to have every advantage.

Thus at the age of 14 Autie entered Alfred Stebbins' "Young Men's Academy," which he attended until it closed two years later. Naturally bright, he seldom did homework but depended on the short periods before each recitation to skim over the lessons of the day. The results always were acceptable.

His deskmate, John Bulkley, loved to recall how young Custer often smuggled novels into class and read them behind the textbook during geography hour. Sly as old Stebbins was, he never was able to catch Autie. The old schoolmaster would pass by in his cloth slippers and pat him on the head with the remark that he was a credit to the school. As soon as he had passed, Autie would lift the end of his geography and return to the heroic charges of the Fourteenth Light Dragoons.

His major interest was reading military novels for even then he had made up his mind to go to West Point. The Mexican War had just closed and most of the heroes had been West Pointers. It was enough to excite any military-minded boy.

Edward Merril, in writing of the time he and Custer were roommates at the Stebbins Academy for a short period, relates how their room was used by the boys as a means of escape for a few hours of fancied liberty after lights were out. Custer was well up in the sports field, always the leader, though a genial and pleasant companion. He did not care too much for boating or swimming but loved and excelled in all other sports.

Much of the time he took care of his half-sister's children. His particular favorite was Harry Armstrong Reed, who was to die with him at the Battle of the Little Big Horn. He too was called *Autie* after his uncle.

It was during this stay in Monroe that he first met the girl who was later to be his wife. Elizabeth Clift Bacon was the only daughter of Monroe's lone judge, Daniel Stanton Bacon. A man of means and position, Judge Bacon had gone a long way since first coming to Monroe. He had been a schoolteacher, a lawyer, a member of the Territorial Leg-

OUT AT THE KNEES. At the age of four Autie (so his family called him) Custer seemed to have difficulty in getting his trouser knees to retain their durability. Mrs. E. B. Custer Collection. Courtesy of the Custer Battlefield Museum.

islature, a judge of probate, a director of a railroad and of a bank. In short, he was a man of character and standing in the community.

On this particular day the freckled, tawny-headed Autie was passing the green-shuttered white house of Judge Bacon's when he was accosted by a pretty dark-eyed girl swinging on the freshly-painted, picket gate. With a dimpled smile she said, "Hello, you Custer boy!" Suddenly frightened at her own boldness she turned and ran into the house. Autie, though living in a world of athletics, never forgot that face.

At the age of 16 Autie returned to Harrison County, Ohio, to teach at the Beech Point School and later at the Locust Grove School, attending McNeely Normal School in Hopedale between terms. Knowing he was deficient in mathematics, it was his desire to strengthen this weakness in order to qualify for West Point. He had applied to Representative John Bingham for the appointment as soon as he had reached New Rumley only to learn that the vacancy already had been filled for that year.

He was well liked by his pupils. He never was known to have any serious difficulty with them for he always was considerate of their problems. Spirited and full of fun, others enjoyed themselves in his presence.

During the first year at Beech Point School, with Capt. Joe Dickerson, he drove a bobsled to get a group of girls for a singing bee. They were so overloaded that Dickerson had to ride on one of the horses. By prearrangement with Custer he took a

sharp turn so fast that all of the girls were thrown into a deep snowbank.

Later while living in a small campus cottage at Hopedale he was attempting to get some sleep in the attic. When some noisy girl visitors below were slow to leave, he thrust his bare feet and legs through the opening in the ceiling as if to come through unclad. In those days of modesty that could have but one effect. The girls left.

Twenty-six dollars a month and board was his pay for teaching. To him that was a small fortune yet he took it all home and placed it in his mother's lap. In later years he spoke of it as one of the happiest moments of his life. He knew they had sacrificed everything to give him the finest education obtainable. It was with a sense of deep gratitude and of love and devotion for their sacrifice that he made this token payment. He knew that if he had placed a million dollars at their feet his debt of gratitude would be only slightly paid.

Chapter Two

EDUCATED FOR WAR

Dad Custer was a staunch old Jacksonian Democrat. He had cast his first vote for General Jackson and, as he stated, "fought it out on that line ever since." It is no small wonder that he was amazed when his son announced he had received an appointment to West Point from the Whig Representative, John A. Bingham.

Years later, Mr. Bingham related how he had received a letter from Custer, then attending school at Hopedale College. "Its honesty captivated me," he said. "It was written in a schoolboy style. In it he said that he understood it made no difference with me whether he was a Whig boy or a Democrat boy—that he wanted me to understand he was a Democrat boy. I replied, if his parents consented, I would procure it for him."

Mother Custer was opposed but Dad Custer and David Reed were in favor of it. Mother soon was won over, however, and Autie was on his way to see Mr. Bingham for some advice as to the problems he would face as a cadet.

In the summer of 1857 Autie landed on the wharf at West Point. He was to be one of a class of 68 plebes admitted that July first. Hazing long had been an extra-curricular activity at the Point, and Custer was no exception to the prevailing rule that all first year students must be "assisted" in their adjustment to plebe life. He was an apt subject and pupil, for many of the tricks played on him he was to redesign if not replace with others more arduous.

He was not the best of students otherwise; his average grades kept him well near the bottom of the class. In his *War Memoirs* he remarks that, "My career as a cadet had but little to commend it to the study of those who came after me, unless as an example to be carefully avoided." His demerits were not obtained through any major offences but made up in number what they lacked in size.

Few generals have graduated high in their class. Generals Grant, "Stonewall" Jackson, Joe Johnson, Joe Hooker, Hancock, Crook, Early, and Sheridan finished well near the foot. Generals George B. McClellan, W. T. Sherman, and Robert E. Lee were outstanding exceptions.

If Autie's record was exceptional, it was so because he stood nearer the foot of the class than at the head. It seems that one hundred demerits for any six-months period would be sufficient to cause dismissal from the academy. Custer had little difficulty in accumulating enough demerits on a number of occasions to bring his total up near the deadline. Unaccustomed to severe restraint, he, like many other cadets, was frequently discovered in his efforts to avoid discipline. It was

WEST POINT FROM FORT PUTNAM. As it appeared in Custer's day. Sketched by B. C. Stone. 1859. Lithographed. by C. Parsons. Author's collection.

not his nature to play mean tricks or to be uncongenial. His demerits in the "Skin book" were principally for tardiness, disorderly uniforms, visiting out of hours, etc.

Friends he had many for he was extremely well liked. And one of the places where all friends met was at Benny Havens; an institution at the Point for many years. Before the Mexican War, Benny Havens had his business inside the lines selling coffee and cakes to the hungry on one hand, and a potent egg-flip to the thirsty on the other. Once discovered by the authorities selling liquor, he was banished from the limits. He re-established his business in a log cabin under a cliff about a mile from the Point, where he specialized in buckwheat cakes and old wine.

It was not the interest in liquor that brought the demerit beggars here so much as the large fund of anecdotes Havens had to offer about the many cadets he knew who had become famous in the service. An added attraction would lie in the thrill of getting out of bounds after taps following a day of irksome discipline.

One of Custer's classmates tells a story of the time Lieutenant Douglas kept a flock of chickens and a buff-colored rooster in a garden just under Custer's window. One night Custer slipped down and took charge of the rooster. After the feast the feathers were carried off. The cadet charged with this responsibility failed to wrap them securely,

consequently there was a trail of yellow feathers leading from Custer's tower-room.

One day in Spanish class Squad Leader Custer opened the period with a request to the instructor to say in Spanish "class dismissed." When the instructor did so, the entire class walked out.

Custer's exuberance and disregard for regulations kept the unsympathetic eyes of his superiors constantly on him. This in no way deterred the adoration of his friends. He was the most popular man in his class.

Nicknamed "Fanny" because of his fair complexion, he excelled as a horseman. The horses assigned were a hard-mouthed, unruly lot since they were constantly changed about. Lessons were given in the riding hall which had a floor strewn with several inches of tanbark. When the order was given to "cross stirrups," almost everyone was thrown, for the McClellan saddles were smooth and difficult to stay in. Custer had the advantage of being long-legged, tall and wiry.

The last year he was at West Point was a trying one for its officials. Not long after December 20. 1860, the Southern States began to secede from the Union. As they did, Southern cadets resigned from the Academy. In that year his class dropped from 57 to 35. The sentiment among Southern cadets was "as the State goes, so must I." It was their feeling that it would have been cowardly to remain in school when their states were in need of their services.

22

Leaving the Academy was painful to many of the Southern boys, yet they were enthusiastic and hopeful. The friends they left behind were reserved and grave. More than three years of extremely close association had built strong bonds.

Though the academic plans called for five years of schooling, the national crisis had created an immediate demand for men with military training. In April of 1861 the course was reduced to four years thereby permitting two classes to graduate that year. The regular class graduated in April and Custer's class was to graduate in June.

Early in June Custer was made officer of the guard. The first day seemed to have progressed uneventfully when at dusk a commotion was heard near the guard tents. Two cadets were fighting over whose turn it was at the water faucet. Quite a crowd of spectators had formed around them by the time Custer arrived. As he tells it, "the instincts of a boy prevailed over the obligation of the officer of the guard. I pushed my way through the surrounding line of cadets, dashed back those who were interfering in the struggle, and called out loudly, "Stand back, boys; let's have a fair fight."

HON. JOHN A. BINGHAM. Though Representative Bingham was a Whig he was above politics for he appointed a Democrat's son (G. A. Custer) to West Point. Courtesy of the Library of Congress.

WITH YOUR PERMISSION MR. PRESIDENT. Here is a portion of Autie's plea as he had written it for his court martial just prior to graduation. 1861. From original in author's collection.

WEST POINT SCHOOL AND BARRACKS. Winter view in 1860. From Schaff's *The Spirit of Old West Point.* Courtesy of Houghton Mifflin Company.

Hardly had he uttered these words when the crowd began to disperse. In looking around to see the cause of this sudden thinning, he observed the appearance of two army officers, Lieutenants Hazen and Merrill. Lieutenant Hazen, who was the officer in charge, asked him why he had not suppressed the "riot." Calling a fist-fight a riot took Custer so by surprise that he was unable to offer an explanation. He realized it was his duty to arrest the two participants and that he had done wrong, but to offer an excuse for not suppressing a riot—that he could not do.

The following morning he was ordered to his tent in arrest and a court-martial was asked to determine the degree of punishment. That same day the long-expected order arrived that relieved his classmates from further duty and permitted them to proceed to Washington for assignment.

On July 15th he was arraigned before a court-martial with as much solemnity as though he were being tried for treason. The trial was brief; he was found guilty and sentenced to be reprimanded in orders.

In the meantime, his many friends interested themselves in his behalf while they were in Washington. The superintendent of the Academy soon received orders to release Custer with instructions to report to the Adjutant General of the Army for duty.

A BOY AND HIS FIRST GUN. Cadet Custer grasps his Colt-Root model as if to use it on the photographer. Circa 1859. Author's collection.

Two days later Custer was in Washington receiving his orders to join the Second Cavalry. The officer in charge asked him if he would like to meet General of the Army Winfield S. Scott. The answer was a spontaneous yes. When General Scott asked him if he wished active duty, he of course gave another affirmative reply and his orders were made out accordingly. He was asked to return again that evening, after he had procured a mount, to carry some dispatches to General McDowell.

Horses were exceedingly scarce but by chance he met a former member of a detachment at West

WEST POINT LIBRARY. Classes were held frequently in these rooms. From Schaff's *The Spirit of Old West Point.* Courtesy of Houghton Mifflin Company.

Point who was getting ready to return an extra horse to a battery near McDowell's forces. He consented to delay his departure until 7 P.M.

Promptly at 7 Custer reported at the Adjutant General's office, obtained his dispatches, and proceeded to the point where he was to pick up the horse. He was agreeably surprised to find it was one of his favorites, a mount he frequently had used during cavalry exercises at West Point.

Custer and his friend rode until nearly 3 o'clock in the morning before they reached the army at Centreville. The men already had breakfasted, and many of the regiments were in marching order, though most of the soldiers were lying down trying to catch a few minutes more sleep.

The road was so filled with soldiers it was with difficulty the horses picked their way over the sleeping forms. Custer's companion knew his way for, dark as it was, he led him right up to General McDowell's headquarters.

An officer challenged him and, when told of the dispatches, asked for them, a request Custer could not decline. He saw him take a few steps toward a half-open tent and place them into the hands of a large, portly officer who he rightly guessed to be General McDowell.

The officer then returned to ask if he desired something to eat. Though Custer was very hungry, he refused for he imagined it unsoldierly to show hunger or fatigue. When asked to dismount and allow his horse to be fed, the offer quickly was accepted. He might go hungry but never would he permit this to happen to any animal in his care.

GRADUATION PICTURE FROM CLASS OF '61 ALBUM. Courtesy of the United States Military Academy Library.

Chapter Three

FIRST ASSIGNMENT

The first battle of Bull Run was about to begin. Less than three days out of West Point and the "shave-tail" was to feel the weight of his newly-acquired rank. He had been assigned to G Company, Second Cavalry, which was found at the head of the column.

The first action began that morning. By 3 in the afternoon, the Confederates were giving way and their every action indicated defeat. Suddenly a column of several thousand fresh troops flanked the half-victorious Federals.

At that moment Custer was standing with a classmate on a high ridge near this point, congratulating each other on the apparent victory. From a distance these troops appeared to be Federal reinforcements. This misconception was quickly erased when they were seen to pour a heavy volley into the backs of the Federal regiments.

Panic seized the Union lines and a demoralized flight began. All attempts to preserve order or retain weapons were disregarded. What could have been their victory became their rout. Years later Custer was to write that:

"One good regiment of such sterling material as made up regiments of either side at the termination of the war, could have checked the pursuit before reaching Bull Run, and could have saved much of the artillery and many of the prisoners."

This battle produced vastly different results in the North and South. The South saw it as a sign of inevitable victory. The North accepted its defeat calmly, then coolly calculated the elements needed to win. The defeat at Bull Run served as a force to unite its many divergencies of opinion and patriotism.

(The North with 23 states had a population of 22,700,000 while the South consisted of 11 states with a population of but 5,096,000.

With the South on the defensive, shorter lines of communication were permissible, greatly aided by its network of rivers. Its chief asset was cotton, but only so if it could be shipped out of the country. Manufacturing was practically non-existent.

The North had ample funds to carry on a war and great variety of manufacturing.

Abraham Lincoln saw the advantage in blockading all the Southern ports and invading Virginia and the Mississippi Valley.

In contrast, Jefferson Davis advocated a policy of defense. This in spite of the advice of

MONROE BUSINESS SECTION DURING THE CIVIL WAR. Custer enjoyed galloping down the board walk in the block beyond on busy days like this. Courtesy of Charles W. Hill. Circa 1863.

THE CUSTER-BACON HOME IN MONROE. The birthplace of Libbie, it now stands five blocks south of its original location where the post office presently stands. The General lived here during the summer of 1868. From a popular Brown and Bigelow calendar of 1910.

COMPARING NOTES. Lieutenants Custer, Jones and Bowen confer in May 1862 near Yorktown. Custer attempts to hide his youthful appearance with sideburns. Photograph by James Gibson. Courtesy of Library of Congress.

"Stonewall" Jackson to invade Maryland and Pennsylvania.)

With the retreating Federal army now safely back near Washington, General George B. McClellan was placed in charge of the demoralized troops. Brigadier General Philip Kearny was given command of volunteers known as the Jersey Brigade. Custer was assigned to him as an aide-de-camp, later becoming his assistant adjutant-general.

Kearny, though a gallant leader, was a martinet to the higher officers. He chafed under the restraint of camp routine, much preferring the action of an attack. Though but briefly on his staff, Custer said of him, "I found him ever engaged in some scheme either looking to the improvement of his command or the discomfiture of his enemy."

Early in the fall of 1861 Custer left Kearney's staff following an order prohibiting officers of the regular army from serving on the staffs of volunteer officers. About this time Brigadier-General Stoneman was made chief of cavalry on the staff of General McClellan. Shortly afterward Custer was attached to Stoneman's outfit. Immediately he was sent home on sick leave, staying in Monroe, Michigan, from October, until February, 1862; then he was assigned to the Fifth Cavalry, Army of the Potomac.

During this stay with his half-sister, Mrs. David Reed, there occurred an event that in later years his wife referred to as "that awful day." While in downtown Monroe he met a few old school friends. Not having seen each other in some years, one drink led to another. Custer, like many others, had thought it manly to drink and swear, now that he was in the army. He had not done so previously for he had been raised in a family of temperate Methodists. Of a nervous and high-strung temperament, he was unable to maintain his stability under its influence. Wending his way down Monroe Street to the Reed home was a problem of using the entire broadwalk for he was no longer able to walk a straight line. One block from his starting point he passed the residence of Libbie Bacon, the girl who two years later would become his wife. Admiring her greatly, but knowing her slightly, it was his misfortune that she should be at a window as he passed. Her observations did not narrow this gap in their acquaintance.

When Mrs. Reed saw she gazed steadily into his eyes for a few moments, picked up the family Bible, then lead him into her bedroom. What transpired there no one knows. But Custer never drank again nor did he use tobacco. He kept his pledge through that fateful day on the Little Big Horn.

When he returned to his post, he did so in a new way of life.

Chapter Four

STEPPING STONE ON THE CHICKAHOMINY

General McClellan had the inescapable task of reorganizing the Army of the Potomac following the Battle of Bull Run. No small part of his problem was to establish morale where none had previously existed. The fact that he had real ability was attested to in Custer's *War Memoirs* in which he states:

> "The impress of McClellan's hand in organizing and preparing the Army of the Potomac for the great task before it, was not only perceptible throughout the period during which McClellan exercised command, but remained with the army through trials to triumph, even up to its last and crowning victory at Appomattox Court-House."

If Custer ever idolized any man, it was McClellan. When McClellan later was to be accused of indecision and unaggressiveness, Custer was foremost among those coming to his defense.

As President, Abraham Lincoln was Commander-in-Chief of the army. Though having no military background, he, like many other presidents, felt a strong urge to meddle in military strategy. It was the President's desire to have McClellan advance immediately on the Confederate forces at Manassas and force another battle of Bull Run. McClellan had other ideas which fortunately prevailed.

It was during the advance on Manassas that Custer was to experience his first charge upon enemy cavalry pickets. The Fifth United States Cavalry, to which he now was assigned, was in the advance. His company was temporarily without a captain and first lieutenant so that when the order to drive the enemy pickets across Cedar Run was received by the regimental commander, Custer asked for and was given permission to drive them back. Thus by accident he was permitted to lead his company in a cavalry charge that drove the enemy pickets out of their way.

Much attention and praise was given this charge, a portion of which was due to a wound received by Private John W. Bryaud. Though not serious, it was the first wound received by the Army of the Potomac.

Lincoln continued to press McClellan to attack even in the face of reducing his command by one-third and removing his control of the base of supplies. With five of his fourteen divisions swept from his command and a chief of engineers advising him not to assault the enemy works because of their strength and character, McClellan refrained from engaging in battle.

A reconnaissance to determine a weak point was unsuccessful. Then it was decided to begin a siege. Young officers were needed to assist the engineering officers engaged in laying out and

MEETING MR. LINCOLN. Custer may be seen at the extreme right as the President confers with General McClellan and his staff during the latter part of 1862. Photograph by Alexander Gardner October 3, 1862. Courtesy of the National Archives.

erecting field works. Since all West Point graduates were supposed to have a practical knowledge of such things, Custer was assigned as assistant to Lieutenant Nicholas Bowen of the Topographical Engineers, until the Army found its advance toward Richmond obstructed by the meandering Chicka-hominy River.

His first assignment was the construction of a riflepit to be used to counteract the annoyance of enemy sharpshooters and artillerymen. This was accomplished overnight with the aid of 100 men. The pit was occupied by two companies of Berdan's sharpshooters, and the annoyance to Federal work parties ceased.

About this time Professor T.S.C. Lowe was receiving considerable attention and ridicule for his introduction of captive balloons for reconnaissance. Since professional balloonists were not considered qualified military observers, General Fitz John Porter had assumed the task. On one occasion, the restraining rope broke releasing both General Porter and the balloon from captivity. Fortunately he remained cool enough to open the escape valve and deflate the balloon sufficiently to permit it to descend. This event cooled the interest somewhat

until young Custer was assigned the task of observer. His commander, General W. F. (Baldy) Smith was so highly satisfied with his observations that he ordered repeated ascensions, particularly in the morning before sunrise and in the evening after sunset.

It was during one of these observations that he noticed the withdrawal of the Confederate forces from the vicinity of Yorktown, a movement that had not been observed by the outposts. The Union army quickly followed to Williamsburg. Custer offered his services to General Hancock, who was leading the pursuit, and was accepted.

In this as in all of his subsequent actions he displayed audacity. It was characteristic that Custer received a commendation for "volunteering and leading the way (in an assault) on horseback."

The South received a serious setback as a result of this Peninsular campaign. Following it, the lower part of the Peninsula was unoccupied by either side after Williamsburg. Most of the fighting thereafter occurred in the neck of the Peninsula just north of Richmond.

By the 22nd of May McClellan had established his headquarters at Coal Harbor about one mile from the Chickahominy River. While the chief of engineers, General Barnard, was reconnoitering he came upon Custer and ordered him to accompany him. Making their way through their picket line they approached the banks of the Chickahominy. Custer was order to jump in, which he instantly did. Finding that the water reached his arm pits and the bottom being slightly muddy but fordable, he kept his revolver above his head and crossed to the other side. Exposed as he was he would have been easy picking for rebel riflemen. Barnard, becoming uneasy because of the nearness of the en-

PROFESSOR T. S. C. LOWE TAKES A LOOK. During the siege of Yorktown, General W. F. (Baldy) Smith ordered Lieutenant Custer to make daily ascensions and observations. Lowe's civilian balloonist had been giving unreliable reports. Because of the poor daytime visibility Custer ascended at night to locate and count the enemy's mess fires. Early one morning he concluded that the enemy had evacuated Yorktown; no fires were visible. General Smith was the first to know. Courtesy of the Library of Congress.

emy pickets, signaled him to return. The young fellow, however, proceeded to examine all the enemy's position, taking note that the main picket post could be cut off by a bold thrust. He then returned to Barnard and reported the river to be fordable. General Barnard returned to McClellan's headquarters and advised him of the reconnaissance. When General McClellan saw Barnard's dry and immaculate uniform, he asked to see the man who had been sent across the river.

Custer was presented to him, wet, muddy and unkempt. Put at ease by McClellan's questioning, he enthusiastically described all that he had observed. The General's response was to ask Custer to become his staff aid-de-camp with the rank of captain. In turn, he requested permission to take some troops over the river and capture the picket posts. This was granted.

On the morning of the attack, he was quite surprised to find that the members of Company A, Fourth Michigan Infantry, assigned to him were all Monroe boys, and many had gone to school with him at Stebbins Academy. Just before sunrise they began the surprise attack on the Louisiana Tigers, driving them down the river. It was Custer who led the attack and personally took a battle flag, the first color ever captured by the Army of the Potomac. Once they had established their bridgehead, he waved to the Federal cavalry to take charge of the splendid opportunity that offered itself. The offer was rejected because the water looked black and dangerous. The Federal cavalry of that time adhered more firmly to prudence than to dash.

Then followed the Seven Days Fight, and the battles at Gaines' Mills and Malvern Hill. Custer took an active role in all of them. These battles

BOYD'S SEMINARY. Libbie Bacon and Margaret Custer attended this Monroe school for girls. A contemporary lithograph from the author's collection.

ended with the Army of the Potomac being forced from the north side of the Peninsula to its south side. It was during this period that Custer was raised to a first lieutenant in the Fifth Cavalry. He still retained the rank of Captain on McClellan's staff until such time as it might be dissolved. It was customary, in certain instances, to retain a permanent rank while carrying a higher rank in performing his temporary duties.

General McClellan was slow to act but fast in losing his prestige with the President and Congress. On November 7th he was succeeded by General Burnside. Since McClellan was placed on "waiting orders" there was nothing left for Custer to do but go home to Monroe for the time being.

The next three months passed pleasurably enough, for it was during this time that he formally met the girl he later was to marry, Libbie Bacon. Nearing her twentieth birthday as well as her graduation from Boyd's Seminary, she was considered the prettiest girl in Monroe.

It was at a Thanksgiving party given by Principal and Mrs. Erasmas Boyd at the seminary where they were introduced. Neither sought to meet the other, yet chance would have it that they did. At first she was not disposed to like him for she remembered "that awful day" earlier that year when she had seen him under the influence of alcohol. He soon overcame her objections, how-

ELIZABETH CLIFT BACON. As she appeared in 1862 following graduation from the Boyd Seminary. Courtesy of the J. C. Custer family.

ever, for he was not one to run from a challenge. Yet in a letter to a friend Libbie wrote, "I don't care for him except as an escort."

In early January of 1863, several weeks prior to his departure to meet McClellan in New Jersey, he was advised to discontinue his visits to the Bacon home for Monroe was beginning to gossip. The Bacon family had objected to the love affair in light of the times for they believed that no good could come from a marriage to a soldier. But it had become obvious the two now were in love.

By mutual agreement his calls were discontinued though they frequently met at parties. When the time came for him to rejoin McClellan, an arrangement was made whereby he would write to their mutual friend Annette Humphrey, and in return would receive all of Libbie's messages through her.

Where there is a will. . . .

MRS. DAVID REED. Lydia Ann Kirkpatrick Reed was a second mother to her half-brother Autie. It was her early influence that had much to do with his temperate habits. From a Monroe (Mich.) newspaper in 1906.

Chapter Five

A STAR WAS GAINED

General McClellan's report was finished in April. Custer was ordered to join his company opposite Fredericksburg. Once again he was Lieutenant Custer.

Following the Union defeat at Chancellorsville, Stoneman was replaced by General Alfred Pleasonton as chief of cavalry. Stoneman had led a successful cavalry raid toward Richmond just prior to his removal, but had failed to attack either Richmond or the two regiments of Confederates that blocked the way. Little of material value was accomplished though it did give the cavalry a "shot in the arm," for this had been the first cavalry success since Antietam.

Captain Custer, for so he found himself in June, was made General Pleasonton's aide-de-camp. It was in this capacity that his true worth first was shown. Tempered for war and mastering the duties of a staff officer in those 18 months since he had been on Kearney's staff, he had highly developed a natural ability to do the right thing at the precise moment it was indicated. His intuitive sense of timing, his judicious application of tactics, and the boundless energy with which he constantly applied himself to all tasks, no matter how minor, made him stand out conspicuously on Pleasonton's staff.

General Pleasonton was an extremely active officer and expected the same from his subordinates. He constanly demanded knowledge of his front and it was the indefatigable Custer who kept him supplied with information of enemy movements and positions. Custer took an active part in every cavalry fight. He made it a personal responsibility to place every picket and did much of the dangerous reconnoitering that carried him across enemy lines.

The cavalry forces under Pleasonton were fast being welded into a fighting force. No longer were they guards and message carriers. They had met the dreaded Stuart's Cavalry and had held their own. More tempering was necessary and then, there would come a day.

On June 9th there had been an engagement at Beverly Ford. It developed that Rebel cavalry forces were concentrating near Culpeper preparatory to a movement around the Union right toward Maryland and Pennsylvania. General Joe Hooker could take his Union forces straight toward Richmond or else fall back to protect Washington. The latter course, though less dramatic, was considered sounder. Lee's forces began pushing up the valley, capturing Winchester on June 13th. It was evident he was to invade Pennsylvania.

Captain Custer, learning that the Seventh Michigan Cavalry needed a colonel, made application to Governor Blair. Though strongly recommended by Generals Hooker, Burnside, Stoneman and

34

NEW BRIGADIER GENERAL 1863. This "reversed glass plate" is the earliest known view of Custer as a brigadier general. Author's collection.

CAVALRY CLASH AT ALDIE, VIRGINIA. During the march toward Gettysburg, the Union cavalry under General Pleasonton met Confederate cavalry under General Stuart. June 24, 1863. Sketch by Edwin Forbes. Library of Congress photo.

Pleasonton, he was rejected by Blair.

On June 16th, Colonel Kilpatrick's cavalry engaged some enemy pickets outside of Aldie. In the battle Stuart drove everything before him in a fierce cavalry charge. When a rout seemed inevitable, Colonels Kilpatrick and Douty dashed out of the massed cavalrymen waving to them to

follow. Custer's biographer Whittaker wrote:

"So great was the turmoil that neither could be heard, when forth from the crowd rode a third figure, a young captain, wearing a broad plantation straw hat, from under which long bright curls flowed over his shoulders. His uniform was careless and shabby, but his bright curls attracted attention wherever he went. Out he rode beside Kilpatrick and Douty, waved his long blade in the air, and pointed to the enemy, then turned his horse and galloped alone toward them. An electric shock seemed to silence the line. He looked back and beckoned with his sword. 'Come on boys,' he shouted."

Kilpatrick and Douty soon were beside him waving their sabres. All fear left the men, and with a shout they rode hard to follow their leaders. For the first time during the war, sabres were used freely. The Confederates dependent on firearms, were unused to this sort of thing. Their only alternative was to drop back. Kilpatrick's horse was shot from under him, and Douty was killed. Custer, stopping for nothing, kept on swinging his sabre every step of the way. At one time he was completely

CAPTURED CLASSMATE. Lieutenant James B. Washington, a West Point classmate, was captured by General McClellan's men. A camp photographer placed this small colored boy in front of them saying, "This ought to be called "Both Sides. The Cause." The picture appeared as such in *Harper's Weekly*. Author's collection.

surrounded by Rebels but managed to escape. He owed it all to the straw hat he wore for, being similar to those worn by the Rebels, he was mistaken for one of them. He made good his escape by cutting down with his sabre one who rushed at him.

Pleasonton sent in the names of Captains Custer, Farnsworth and Merritt, with that of Colonel Kilpatrick, for promotion to the rank of Brigadier General. On June 29th Custer received notice of his appointment, just two days before the Battle of Gettysburg. Of all the assignments in this newly-reorganized Army of the Potomac, he was to command all of what he had been refused a part, the Michigan Cavalry Brigade. On the day of his appointment he joined them at Hanover, Pennsylvania.

The GI uniform of that period was a sloppy, unpretentious thing. Custer did a bit of refashioning by lowering the crown of the black hat and widening the brim. Next, he discarded the tight cavalry jacket and replaced it with a loose black velvet one, with trousers to match. Velvet was frequently used because of its strength and it also gave a rich effect. To set off the jacket he had braids of gold lace running up the sleeves almost to his shoulders. Utilizing the broad-collared blue shirt of the navy, he indicated his rank of brigadier by placing a silver star in each corner of the collar. A scarlet necktie was at his throat. To complete the picture of a well-dressed cavalier, he thrust his loose trousers into the tops of his high boots.

In this dress he assumed his new command. This foppish youth with the yellow curls already had jumped, along with Merritt and Farnsworth, over the seniority of other men. Pleasonton had endangered his own future by recommending these boys. Advancing them over the heads of his overcautious colonels and generals had created much jealousy. So Custer took command with "two strikes" on him.

His first step was to choose a staff from his own brigade, selecting old Monroe acquaintances. He had to act cool and distant to his colonels for he realized that to be friendly would encourage them to clap him on the back and give him advice. The only way to obtain the confidence of his men was to be through the welding fire of battle. That opportunity soon would be at hand.

General JEB Stuart, chief of the Confederate cavalry, had started his men for Carlisle, Pennsylvania. Passing through Hanover on June 29th he struck the rear of Farnsworth's column, capturing his pack train. In turn Farnsworth countercharged, checking Stuart's progress for that day.

Meanwhile General Fitzhugh Lee's brigade had been sighted one mile south of Hanover. The Sixth Michigan under Colonel George Gray repulsed three of their charges, then retired from the field. The result of this contact was to cause Stuart to detour to the east away from Lee, who was nearing Gettysburg, the Union cavalry holding the inside of the circle. It was not until Stuart reached Carlisle that he obtained the first reliable information of Lee's whereabouts. He was not able to reach Lee's main army until late in the day of July 2, the battle then having finished its second day, with the outcome still in doubt.

While Custer's brigade was leading the Third Division toward Hunterstown it encountered a heavy force of Confederate cavalry. After a spirited affair of nearly two hours the enemy was driven back with considerable loss, for which the Sixth Michigan Cavalry and Pennington's battery received official commendation. This position near Hunterstown was held until midnight when Kilpatrick received orders to move some five miles southeast of Gettysburg to Two Taverns. Custer bivouacked at 3 a.m.

The rolling thunder and quaking earth that announced the cannonading that preceded Picket's charge started around 2 p.m. Shortly afterward Custer gave the signal for Colonel Russell Alger to advance and engage the enemy. They moved from

THE CHARGE AT ALDIE. Leading the charge that gave Confederate General J. E. B. Stuart his first cavalry defeat had much to do with Custer being awarded a general's star. Sketch by A. R. Waud, June 16, 1863. From Whittaker's *A Complete Life of Gen. George A. Custer.*

GENERAL PLEASONTON'S PERSONAL AIDS. Custer is seated at the extreme right and General Pleasonton is seated next to him, 1863. Mrs. E.B. Custer collection. Custer Battlefield Museum.

field to field and fence to fence until a line of gray came out from behind the Rummel farm buildings and the woods nearby. Though superior in numbers, the gray line gave way to the heavier fire power provided by the Wolverines' Spencer repeating carbines. In turn, Stuart's reinforcements moved forward when the wasteful Spencers had used up all the ammunition.

Alger, compelled to retire, ordered his men to their horses. The men in gray followed in quick pursuit. Suddenly a column of mounted men was seen to advance from the Union lines. Gregg knowing the necessity for prompt action, had ordered the Seventh Michigan ready for a charge. As it moved forward, Custer drew his sabre, dashed in front of them and shouted: "Come on you Wolverines!" On they rode, straight at the dismounted line of rebels, which broke and ran for the rear. When half way, Custer turned to the left, the regiment sailing on under its own leaders. By accident the column was deflected into a post-and-rail fence. Under terrific fire they regrouped and resumed the charge up to another fence some 200 yards from the enemy batteries.

By this time the Ninth and Thirteenth Virginia cavalries had opened the fence and struck the flank of the Seventh Michigan. The Seventh Michigan then counter-attacked, and while retiring it was struck in the flank by a mounted charge of the First Virginia cavalry, this in turn was met and driven back by the Fifth Michigan under Colonel Alger. Then there was a pause.

Two of Stuart's choice brigades had been kept in reserve. Regiment by regiment they emerged from the woods northeast of the Rummel buildings and took their places. Suddenly Pennington opened up with all six of his rifled cannons. Great gaps were torn in the columns of mounted men in gray, and were as quickly closed. Generals Wade Hampton and Fitzhugh Lee led a sabre charge as Pennington continued a murderous fire with double cannister. Still they advanced. The Fifth, Sixth and Seventh Michigans had drawn to one side, ready. Then Gregg rode over to the First Michigan ordering Colonel Charles Town to charge. Custer, who had dashed over with similar instructions, placed himself at the side of Town, in front of the leading squadron.

Led by Custer and Town, they started at a trot. When the command to charge was given, they hurled themselves at the Gray column, while the Fifth struck the right flank and the Sixth and Seventh charged the left. The Gray staggered under the blows to its flanks but it was Town's charge that went through it like a knife, scattering the gray horsemen like ten-pins. Stuart called his disorganized men together, leaving the field to the Wolverines.

Thus ended the cavalry fighting on the Union's right flank at Gettysburg. Considered by military

38

analysts as the finest cavalry charge made during the Civil War, one wonders what might have happened to the soft under-belly of Meade's forces on Cemetery Ridge, being the very center of the Union defense position, had Stuart succeeded in routing Gregg's brigade during this charge, and enabling him to strike the Union's practically undefended rear.

MAJOR GENERAL IRVIN McDOWELL. Commanding officer of the Union forces at the first Battle of Bull Run, Custer's first engagement. Courtesy of the Library of Congress.

WITH THE MAN WHO MADE HIM GENERAL. Captain Custer and his chief, Major General Alfred Pleasonton pose at Brandy Station, Va. It was soon after this that Pleasonton recommended Custer's appointment to a brigadier generalcy. Photo by Brady, June, 1863.

39

LATER THAT YEAR. There is some modification in dress and hair length. 1863.
Courtesy of Custer Battlefield Museum.

Chapter Six

FIGHTING WAS HIS BUSINESS

Near the end of the following day, July 4th, Custer's brigade contacted the rear of Lee's retreating forces and captured his wagon train near Monterey Gap. Custer had his seventh horse shot from under him in this campaign.

The rebels were pursued and harassed in a manner seldom employed previously. Tempering audacity with discretion, Custer used mounted charges against equal or inferior forces, and dismounted skirmishers for defensive action against superior numbers.

In the subsequent battle at Falling Waters he used his entire brigade against four enemy brigades behind earthworks. The result of his charge was the capture of the entire First Brigade of twelve hundred men. Custer was satisfied with that but Kilpatrick, who came up at this point, ordered his men on with the hopes of capturing the other three brigades. Of the one hundred men who made the charge only thirty remained who were unwounded, for the surrendering brigade took up their arms again and began a fierce resistance. Custer had known the limits of audacity; Kilpatrick had not.

Falling Waters ended the Gettysburg campaign, for Lee had crossed the Potomac into Virginia. Following several lesser engagements in September, Custer led a successful charge at Culpeper in which his horse was killed by a shell fragment and he was painfully though not seriously wounded in the thigh. It enabled him to return to Monroe for twenty days.

Custer had proposed to Libbie Bacon the previous winter but she had not realized that she loved him until that Spring. So he took up where he had left off, and it was under a tree in the Bacon garden that they made their pledge. Libbie held that there should be no formal engagement until her father's ungrudging consent was obtained. When the Judge learned that Custer was to make a formal application for her hand, he suddenly found business requiring his attention in Traverse City. Relenting, he returned in time to see Custer off at the station, but gave him no opportunity to open the subject.

Not back to his command two days he had two horses shot from under him in the fierce engagement at Brandy Station. At one time during this engagement he found some 5,000 rebels in front of him so, raising up in his stirrups, he yelled out, "Boys of Michigan, there are some people between us and home; I'm going home. Who else goes?" The men responded with three cheers, and were additionally inspired when the brigade band struck up "Yankee Doodle." It is almost needless to add that the sabre charge was successful.

Though October was occupied with a number of skirmishes and a pitched battle with Stuart at

CHARGE OF THE SIXTH MICHIGAN AT FALLING WATERS. Cavalry charge over the rebel earthworks in the last battle of the Gettysburg campaign, July 14, 1863. Sketch by A. R. Waud. Courtesy of Library of Congress.

Buckland Mills, Custer still found time to write Judge Bacon for the privilege of corresponding with Libbie. He wrote of his vow to his sister followed by two years temperance, and that he always had had a purpose in life. Near the end of the month Libbie wrote to him:

"My more than friend—at last—am I a little glad to write you some of the thoughts I cannot control. I have enjoyed your letters to Nettie, (Annette Humphrey was Libbie's closest friend), but am delighted to possess some of my own."

Judge Bacon had given his consent, even chiding his daughter about keeping Custer waiting. Custer had long been patient and now was being rewarded for it. Though a spring wedding had been planned, they soon decided on an earlier date. On February 9, 1864, they took their vows at the Presbyterian Church in Monroe. A short honeymoon to Cleveland, Buffalo and West Point, and then back to his brigade headquarters at Stevensburg.

Preparations were under way for a raid toward Richmond. Kilpatrick had ordered Custer, Gregg and Merritt to select special cavalry detachments and provide them with several days rations. Moving

ARTILLERY HURRYING TO THE FRONT AT BRANDY STATION, VIRGINIA. A light artillery battery hurrying to the front near Culpeper Court House in pursuit of Stuart's cavalry, September 1863. Sketch by Edwin Forbes. Courtesy of Library of Congress.

CAVALRY CHARGE NEAR BRANDY STATION—1863. Sketch by Edwin Forbes, 1864. Courtesy of Library of Congress.

THE FIFTH MICHIGAN AT OPEQUAN Winchester. A charge of one of Custer's regiments. Sketch by A. R. Waud, Sept. 19, 1864. Courtesy of Library of Congress.

out, on February 28th, with 5,000 cavalrymen, they succeeded in cutting off several railroads between General Lee and Richmond but failed in their main objective of freeing the Union prisoners at Richmond.

Spring saw General Grant made chief of staff, and Phil Sheridan as chief of cavalry. Preparations soon were under way for what was to result in the Battle of the Wilderness. Custer's Wolverines, becoming the First Brigade of the First Division, broke camp on the morning of May 4th. Two days later they were attacked by the cavalry forces of his old West Point classmate, General Tom Rosser, whom he repulsed with great skill. Though Sheridan was given all credit he was not on the field at any time. General Kidd writes that, "it was Custer's attack and Custer's victory."

Sheridan now had acquired the habit of placing the Michigan Brigade at the head of his advancing column when any serious work had to be done. Custer had designated the First Michigan as a sabre regiment as it was his oldest in experience and had the more daring officers. The Seventh Michigan was its understudies. In turn the Fifth and Sixth were used for dismounted action when in contact with the enemy. This soon became second nature to all of them. They worked very well together and had no superiors on the skirmish line.

TREVILLIAN STATION CAVALRY BATTLE. In this engagement on June 12, 1864 the Michigan Cavalry Brigade under General Custer is being struck in the rear by General Thomas L. Rosser and his Virginia Cavalry Brigade. Rosser, Custer's class and roommate at West Point, may be seen in the center swinging his hat in the air just before his leg was broken by a carbine ball. Custer may be seen in the right center reaching for his own colors as they fall from the hands of his mortally wounded Sergeant Harrison Blevir. Painted by James E. Taylor, 1881. Courtesy of Custer Battlefield Museum.

Sheridan was out after Stuart's forces for he knew if he could destroy the Confederate cavalry corps the end would not be far away. He had told General Meade he could whip Stuart in a fair fight if given the chance. Meade reported this conversation to Grant who told him to let Sheridan try it. Sheridan loaded his guns.

By forced marches General Stuart managed to reach Yellow Tavern on May 11th, ahead of Sheridan. The former was pushed back several hundred yards to the east of the turnpike by General Merritt but Stuart's enfilade created considerable damage. Custer then made a mounted attack upon the enemy's left and battery. "Custer's charge," according to Sheridan in his MEMOIRS, . . . "was brilliantly executed. Beginning at a walk, he increased his gait to a trot, and then at full speed rushed at the enemy." The Confederates were driven across the Chickahominy River, their chief of cavalry, JEB Stuart, dead of wounds received from one of Custer's men.

Following this engagement there were numerous raids and skirmishes ending with the two-day battle of Trevillian Station on June 11th and 12th which Sheridan thought to be the most brilliant cavalry engagement of that particular campaign. Most of June and July was used to rest the men and horses. By mid-August the men were ready. Off they went on a series of actions. There was much marching, counter-marching, picketing, skirmishing and reconnoitering.

Grant had observed that Lee's raids had not gone over the bare lands of Bull Run but up the rich valley of the Shenandoah. He resolved to strip this valley bare and an order went out to that effect. In the early part of September the cavalry was constantly used in harassing the enemy. Since their adversaries were principally infantrymen, they soon became adept in attacks on infantry lines. On the 19th of September the engagement at Winchester began. Here again Custer displayed a more-than-ordinary ability to make decisions for a brigade

45

GENERAL J. E. B. STUART. Stuart was the flower of the Confederate cavalry and a superb cavalryman. He was a thorn in the side of the Union for he never met his match until he came against Custer. He met his death at Yellow Tavern attempting to repel a charge of the Michigan Cavalry Brigade led by Custer. Courtesy Library of Congress.

46

while under fire. When the battle was over, Custer's command of about 500 officers and men captured more than 700 men, 52 officers, 7 battleflags and numerous small arms. For gallant and meritorious service Custer was made a Major General of Volunteers, and placed in command of the Second Division in place of Averill. Four days later, before he had had time to join his new command, he was placed in command of the Third Division, which included his crack Michigan Brigade.

The rebels now were concentrating down near the end of the Shenandoah Valley, indicating their intention of opposing any movement toward Richmond. Sheridan's men had destroyed everything in the valley that would be of any value to the enemy. The order to fall back was given on October 6th, the cavalry bringing up the rear, Merritt taking the valley pike and Custer the east slope of the Little North Mountain. The destruction was continued while Generals Lomax and Rosser followed and gave them continual trouble with their gunfire. On the morning of the 9th Sheridan ordered his officers to either whip the Confederate cavalry or get whipped.

GENERAL LOMAX MISSES HIS MAIL. Gen. J. E. B. Stuart's mail seemed to get into Custer's mailbox quite frequently. Sept. 22, 1863. Author's collection.

TAKING THE ENEMY GUNS. Custer's Cavalry in action at Culpeper Court House, Va., September 14, 1863. Sketch by Edwin Forbes. Courtesy of Library of Congress.

GENERAL CUSTER AND PLEASONTON. Custer confers with his chief at Warrenton, Va. in October 1863. Photo by Alexander Gardner, October 1863. Courtesy of Library of Congress.

Custer received this order with joy for he had enough of retreat, with men under his old classmate Rosser constantly harassing his rear guard. The rolling surface of the valley presented an ideal place for a cavalry fight. With no rail fences intervening and ample room to deploy, Custer gave the order for a sabre charge, for Rosser was directly on his front. Sweeping down on him in full sight, he had him surrounded with a semi-circle of horsemen before he realized what had happened.

The Confederates were thrown into immediate confusion for they were at a standstill depending upon their fire to halt the charge. Behind them was an open field—their only avenue of escape. Retreat, they did; sometimes at a gallop, and sometimes at a walk, fleeing to Mount Jackson twenty-six miles away. Though officially known as the Battle of Tom's Brook it was frequently referred to as *The Woodstock Races.*

Ten days later occurred the Battle of Cedar Creek which might have been a Federal defeat but for the timely arrival of Sheridan. Following this battle, little of importance occurred during the winter of 1864-65. On the last day in February Custer took part in a very successful thrust toward Richmond. This was but one of a series of engagements—Five Forks, South Side Railroad, Namozine Church, Saylor's Creek—and then, Appomattox Court House.

These were cavalry days, Custer days, for he was usually in the lead, and in the thick of every action. It was time for audacity, quick decision, and immediate action. Custer always was in the advance, always in motion in front of his men. While Devin was watching his own lines, Custer was up in front

CAPTURED FIELD ORDER—GENERAL R. E. LEE. One can readily imagine Custer's delight at intercepting such an order. Author's collection.

Custer's Luck they called it. This word "luck" was applied to many other things concerning him. He always seemed to win his battles, by luck, his critics said. When *they* won, is was by genius.

On the morning of April 9, 1865, just as Custer was about to lead a charge, a rider from the opposing lines bearing a white towel hailed Custer. Custer accepted it and investigated. Lee had surrendered.

Later that day, after the surrender terms had been signed, he sat down and drafted a farewell to his beloved Third Cavalry Division. It read, in part:

"During the past six months, although in most instances confronted by superior numbers, you have captured from the enemy in open battle, one hundred and eleven pieces of artillery, sixty-five battle-flags and upwards of ten thousand prisoners, including seven general officers. . . . You have never lost a gun, never lost a color, and have never been defeated. . . ."

GENERAL CUSTER. 1864. Photo by Brady. Courtesy of National Archives.

where he could watch the enemy lines.

He was a different looking Custer now that he had that second star. The velvet jacket was gone, replaced by one of blue sack with the major-general's shoulder boards. His trousers were of the regulation sky-blue. The old blue shirt, the cavalier hat, the long curls, and the red necktie still remained. He still could be seen by his men, and the enemy. Yet he had been wounded but once.

CAPTURED FIELD ORDER—GENERAL J. E. B. STUART. Discovered amongst General Custer's papers. Author's collection.

GENERAL CUSTER. Taken shortly after his wedding. Photo by Brady, 1864. Courtesy of National Archives.

GENERAL CUSTER. 1864. Photo by Brady. Courtesy of National Archives.

MAJOR GENERAL CUSTER. The second star was awarded for gallant and meritorious services in the winter campaigns of 1864. Brady photo about 1865. Courtesy of National Archives.

MAJOR GENERAL CUSTER. Brady photo about 1865. Courtesy of National Archives.

BATTLE ATTIRE. No one could mistake the commanding officer when Custer rode in front of his troops. Attired in blue as pictured, with red necktie and yellow curls in contrast, neither his men nor the enemy could doubt who was leading his cavalry charge. Brady photo about 1865. Courtesy of National Archives.

THE BOY GENERAL. The youngest general in the United States Army at the time, Custer realized that his youthful appearance was a hindrance according to all standards of leadership. First he tried sideburns, then a flowing mustache with small goatee, as in the picture above. Later, he retained only his mustache. Brady photo about 1865. Courtesy of National Archives.

"OLD CURLY." An affectionate nickname adopted by the men in the ranks under him. Brady photo about 1865. Courtesy of Custer Battlefield Museum.

GENERAL PHILIP SHERIDAN AND STAFF. Left to right: Generals Sheridan, Forsyth, Merritt, Devin, and Custer, 1864. Mrs. E. B. Custer Collection. Custer Battlefield Museum.

SHERIDAN AND HIS GENERALS. Young and vigorous, they were the core of Sheridan's striking power. 1864. Mrs. E. B. Custer Collection. Custer Battlefield Museum.

PRISONERS BEING CAPTURED BY THE MICHIGAN CAVALRY BRIGADE. Custer's cavalry at work in Winchester, Va., September 19, 1864. A. R. Waud sketch. Courtesy of the Library of Congress.

AUDACITY, ALWAYS AUDACITY. Custer prepares for his third charge at Sailer's Creek. His constant hammering of the rebel forces played a major part in the final phase of the war near Appomattox Court House. A. R. Waud sketch, April 6, 1865. Courtesy of Library of Congress.

CUSTER'S CAPTURED FLAGS. Artist A. R. Waud's sketch made at the presentation of the flags in Washington and used in *Harper's Weekly* as a front page illustration. Courtesy of Library of Congress.

CAPTURED CONFEDERATE FLAGS. On October 23, 1864 General Custer presented to the Secretary of War the battle-flags captured from the Confederates at the Battle of Cedar Creek. During this Washington ceremony it was announced that Custer had been appointed a Major General. From A. R. Waud's sketch in *Harper's Weekly*.

Custer receiving the flag of truce appomatox — 186

THE END WAS NEAR. The flag of truce Custer received from the Confederate forces near Appomattox Court House is displayed in the museum there. Though he was an observer of the surrender ceremony in the McLean house he was not a participant. A. R. Waud sketch. Courtesy of Library of Congress.

JUST A DOG AND HIS MASTER. Taken at field headquarters while with the Army of the Potomac. While in the West after the war Custer frequently kept a dozen dogs and as many wild pets. Brady photograph. Courtesy of the Custer Battlefield Museum.

RECEIVING THE FLAG OF TRUCE. Custer was in the advance with his division when an officer from the Confederate lines galloped toward him waving a towel tied to a branch. A. R. Waud sketch from *A Complete Life of Gen. George A. Custer.*

SURRENDER TOWEL. Custer retained this towel of truce after he had reported to his superior General Sheridan that General Lee had thrown up the white flag. Photo by J. G. Hill in author's collection.

1864 HEADQUARTERS NEAR WINCHESTER, VIRGINIA. Photo by Bowlsby in Mrs. E. B. Custer Collection Custer Battlefield Museum.

CUSTER'S HEADQUARTERS. This house is thought to be near Stevensburg, Virginia, 1864. Mrs. E. B. Custer Collection, courtesy of Custer Battlefield Museum.

SURRENDER AT APPOMATTOX. The room in the McLean House at Appomattox Court House, Virginia in which General Lee surrendered to General Grant. General Custer stands in the left foreground, General Lee sits in the chair to the left and General Grant sits next to him. General Sheridan stands between the two chairs. From a lithograph in author's collection published by Major & Knapp, 1867.

McLEAN HOUSE AT APPOMATTOX COURT HOUSE, VIRGINIA. This house has been completely reconstructed by the National Park Service. To the left of the center door is the room in which Generals Grant and Lee drafted and signed the peace terms April 9, 1865. Courtesy of Library of Congress.

LIEUT. GENERAL GRANT AT CITY POINT. Near the James River in August 1864.
Courtesy of Library of Congress.

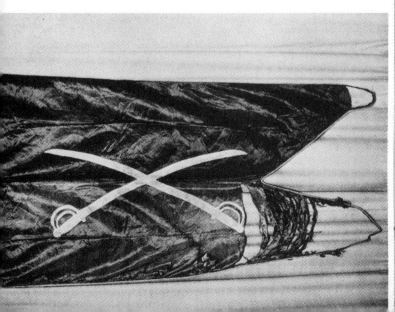

Appomattox Court House
April 10th 1865

My Dear Madam

Respectfully present to you the small writing table on which the Conditions for the Surrender of the Confederate army of Northern Virginia was written by Lt Genl Grant ... permit me to say Madam that there is scarcely an individual in our service who has contributed more to bring about this desirable result than your very gallant husband.

Very respectfully
Phil H. Sheridan
Maj Genl

Mrs Genl Custer
Washington D.C.

SHERIDAN'S LETTER. Appomattox Court House, April 10th, 1865. Photo by J. G. Hill of Monroe, Michigan. in author's collection.

THE GRANT SURRENDER TABLE. This is the table upon which General Grant drafted the terms for the surrender of the Confederate army. It was purchased from Mr. McLean by General Sheridan for twenty dollars in gold and presented to Mrs. Custer. Photo by J. G. Hill in author's collection.

GENERAL CUSTER'S PERSONAL FLAG. Red and blue silk with crossed sabres in white on both sides and edged with heavy white cording, it had been made by Mrs. Custer's hands. Author's collection.

REST IN MONROE. Custer was wounded in the thigh at Culpeper Court House, Virginia. He returned to Monroe in October 1863 to recuperate, and court Libbie Bacon. This may explain the clean-shaven face. 1863. Brady photo. Courtesy of National Archives.

SECOND LIEUTENANT THOMAS WARD CUSTER. Tom Custer managed to get transferred from the Ohio Volunteers to the Michigan Volunteers. He was made an aide on his brother's staff, joining it at Winchester. He wears the red tie of the Wolverines. Mrs. E. B. Custer Collection, Custer Battlefield Museum.

Chapter Seven

THE GIRL HE LEFT BEHIND

Elizabeth Clift Bacon was no ordinary woman. Though brought up in luxury it was her wish to share the hardships of camp life just to be near her husband. Destined to a life of repeated separations, she kept up a continuous correspondence with him during each one to help lessen their loneliness.

Following their honeymoon she returned to the brigade headquarters at Stevensburg with him. Prior to her arrival the presence of a respectable woman around the army practically was unknown. It was the prevailing belief that the camp was no place for ladies, especially if they wished to remain respectable. After a short time it was observed that her presence had a restraining influence upon the men. Vulgarity and drunkenness became uncommon around headquarters. The officers' wives quickly learned of the improved conditions and soon joined their husbands.

Living in a requisitioned farmhouse the Custers managed a degree of elegant living. Though most of the officers' wives rode around in ambulances, Custer bought Libbie two horses to draw a carriage (with silver harness) he had captured the previous summer. It usually was escorted by four or six cavalrymen.

When Spring came, the cavalry raids were to begin. Custer took Libbie to Washington to remain there until he had a more permanent camp. The short time they spent there together was full of excitement for Libbie. Meeting the President, many important generals, senators, and congressmen, all of whom spoke to Custer in the most complimentary manner about his exploits, amazed her and gave her a sense of pride she could not help writing about to her father.

When it came time for her husband to leave she watched him admiringly as he rode away, but once out of sight she went up to her room to cry. She was far lonelier than she had anticipated though she wrote her mother and father she was prouder of being his wife than being either Mrs. Lincoln or a queen.

Late in April she attended a Presidential reception and while in the Blue Room had just shaken hands with President Lincoln and was passing on, when her name was mentioned. With this the President took her hand and shook it again very cordially saying, "So this is the young woman whose husband goes into a charge with a whoop and a shout. Well, I'm told he won't do so anymore." She replied that she hoped he would. "Oh," he said, "then you want to be a widow, I see." With which they both laughed.

The *Boy General,* for so the press now called him, kept a continual stream of correspondence

HEADQUARTERS NEAR WINCHESTER, VIRGINIA. 1. General Custer; 2. Mrs. General Custer; 3. Judge Daniel S. Bacon; 4. Mrs. Judge Bacon; 5. Mrs. Dr. Wood; 6. Dr. Wood; 7. Captain Lee; 8. Lieut. D. Norval; 9. James Christiancy; 10. Baron Sieb; 11, Fred Nims; 12. Miss Rebecca Richmond; 13. Lt. Tom Custer; 14. General Whitaker; 15. Bugler Joseph Fought; 16. Henry Mail; 17. B. Marshall. Author's collection.

JUDGE ISAAC P. CHRISTIANCY. One of Custer's closest friends. From an engraving by H. B. Hall and Sons.

flowing toward Libbie. Addressing her as "My Durl" or similar pet phrases, she kept well informed as to the operations of his cavalry unit. Constantly admonishing her not to show any of the numerous news clippings about himself, he would reconstruct entire engagements for her from first-hand knowledge. Occasionally he would allude to his lessened use of profanity during battle, all because of her splendid influence.

She, in turn, would write of the progress with her sewing and of the happenings in Washington. Included were her dreams of their future family (a boy and a girl), and of her joy at hearing that he had successfully overcome the habit of using oaths during the heat of battle.

Time was almost a burden to Libbie while she lived in Washington. Because she was the attractive wife of an officer extremely well known, life became a bit difficult at times when elderly men of great political standing would sometimes feel kittenish in her presence. She would gravely write her husband of the incident and of the unoffending manner with which the advances were rejected.

Judge and Mrs. Bacon were the happy recipients of her long and informative letters. She would tell them, of her enjoyment of church, and of her studied plainness of dress so as to avoid appearing like *women of a certain class*.

During ths period, Jim Christiancy, a Monroe boy on Custer's staff, was wounded seriously. Libbie had brought him to her boarding house where she could nurse him back to health for she thought the Washington hospitals too unbearable for him. Jim did

GENERAL AND MRS. CUSTER. This is thought to be the first picture of the two together. Photo by Brady, 1864. Courtesy of National Archives.

LIBBIE'S WEDDING GOWN. Her first thought was to have a simple wedding, but, like many others with similar plans, simplicity was soon forgotten. 1864. Courtesy of J. C. Custer family.

well under her care for she recognized his need for the influence of a good Christian woman. He had been a protégé of Custer's through the influence of his friend, Judge Isaac Christiancy, father of the boy. Jim was the alcoholic scapegrace of the fine Christiancy family.

Late in October of 1864, soon after Custer was made a major general, he was sent to Washington to deliver captured battle-flags to the Secretary of War. After the presentation Mr. Stanton asked if his father was Emanuel Custer. When assured that he was, Stanton told him that Emanuel once had been his client. He had wondered if there was any relationship but had discounted the idea when he discovered Custer was from Michigan.

Libbie met Custer at Martinsburg, Virginia, that November, a short time later moving on to Winchester. Here they were joined by brother Tom Custer who had just been transferred from an Ohio unit. Tom added much family spirit to the reunion for, though an excellent soldier, he was full of fun and practical jokes. He was to be awarded *two* Medals of Honor during the Civil War; the only person in any branch of the service so honored.

At Winchester the time passed rapidly for Libbie even though her General went out on frequent raiding parties. Here she was to learn that her husband's interests were varied. He had a great love for animals and particularly loved dogs and horses. They greatly enjoyed watching his pet coon and pet squirrel play together. Before returning to Washington, she learned from Lieutenant Fred Nims, one of her husband's aides, that it was Autie's custom to offer a prayer before entering any battle.

Once in Washington she set about to make Autie a personal headquarters flag. It was a forked pennant of half red and half blue silk, with crossed white sabres on both sides, and edged with heavy white cord. Carried with him through the balance of the war, it was the same kind of flag he had when he received that fatal bullet on the Little Big Horn River twelve years later.

Once the surrender terms were signed at Appomattox Court House, General Sheridan gave Mr. McLean, (owner of the house in which the surrender terms were completed) twenty dollars in gold for the small, pine varnished table upon which General Grant had drafted and signed the surrender terms. He immediately gave the table to

General Custer to be presented to Libbie with a note that read:

Appomattox Court House
April 10, 1865.

My dear Madam,

I respectfully present to you the small writing-table on which the conditions for the surrender of the Confederate Army of Northern Virginia were written by Lt. General Grant—and permit me to say, Madam, that there is scarcely an individual in our service who has contributed more to bring about this desirable result than your very gallant husband.

Mrs. Genl. Custer
Washington, D.C.

Very Respectfully,
Phil H. Sheridan
Major General.

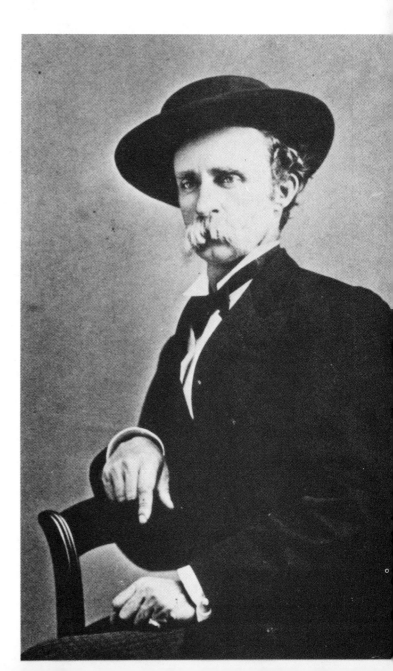

THE GENERAL'S WEDDING DAY. Civilian clothes were worn on the honeymoon toward West Point. Mrs. E. B. Custer collection. Courtesy of Custer Battlefield Museum.

GENERAL AND MRS. CUSTER WITH BROTHER TOM. The three were almost inseparable. Brady photo. Courtesy of National Archives.

Chapter Eight

THE PATH TO RECONSTRUCTION

The war was over. There was nothing to keep Libbie from her husband now. A woman in love sees no obstacles, for Libbie reached Richmond ahead of her husband, who had spent four years in getting there.

Libbie rode to Petersburg and then on to Washington in an ambulance, happy to again be with the army. By the middle of May she was able to view an encampment of two hundred thousand veterans on the south side of the Potomac at the very edge of the capital.

The Grand Review was held on May 23rd and 24th. General Sheridan was gone for he had been ordered toward impending trouble on the Rio Grande. Major General Merritt assumed command of the cavalry which headed the column of the marching Army of the Potomac as it passed in review before the President. Nearing the reviewing stand on Pennsylvania Avenue it drew its sabres. Recognizing Custer, a group of 300 white-clad girls sang "Hail To The Chief," at the same time throwing wreaths and bouquets at him.

> Whittaker states that, "The sudden rush, the pelting of bouquets and the peal of the 300 voices frightened his steed (Don Juan, a thoroughbred race horse), and before he could gather up the reins the excited animal made the rush we saw from the other end of the Avenue. As the gallant general flew past the President's stand he bethought him to salute Johnson and Gen. Grant, but in doing so, in the rush his sabre caught in his wide hat, and sabre and headgear fell to the ground. Then with his long, yellow, curly hair floating out behind, he settled himself in the saddle as if he grew there, and by one of the most magnificent exhibitions of horsemanship he in a moment reined in the flying charger, and returned to meet his troops."

Custer was not to see the end of the Grand Review for he had orders to go to Texas. Leaving his men of the Third Division was a painful ordeal but once on the train for Louisville he became impatient because of the slow pace with which they moved. From Louisville the leisurely boat trip to New Orleans did much to becalm his battle-worn nerves. New Orleans was a delightful place for Libbie and him to explore but after a short stay they took a boat up the Red River for Alexandria. It was here that he and his staff had many weeks of hard work in organizing a division of cavalry for the march to Texas.

Most of his 4,000 men were volunteers who, during the war, were, to all intents and purposes, regulars. They had enlisted for three years or the duration, and now that the war was over, wanted to go home. This jaunt to Louisiana and Texas was not to their liking and they intended showing their displeasure. But the officers, who were receiving good pay, were contented with their lot.

Some of the regiments in this command never fired a gun in the entire war. What they needed

VICTORIOUS ARMY. May 24 and 25, 1865 saw Washington's Pennsylvania Avenue crowded with happy civilians and soldiers. Courtesy of Library of Congress.

was the regimental pride that was gained by the bond of battle. They received every order with grumbles and growls, and it soon became the custom of some officers to explain to their men the reasons for each order.

One of the colonels became greatly disturbed when, on the preceding night, his tent had been riddled by the gunfire of his men, from which he might have been killed but for his lying flat on the ground.

Soon after arriving at Alexandria, the men began deserting, going out on unauthorized raids, and robbing indiscriminately. They seemed to have no feeling for the rights of the conquered.

General Custer was under orders to treat the civilians with every consideration. Orders were given to his officers accordingly.

One particular officer created so much dislike for himself that his men threatened him, then drew up and signed a petition demanding his resignation. This was mutiny.

On Custer's demand, all apologized and were restored to duty but one. This lone sergeant refused to admit he was wrong. He immediately was court martialed and sentenced to be shot. His former associates became seriously concerned about him for he was a family man. A petition was presented asking for his pardon, but this the General denied.

70

Now the men were worked up. Threats of every kind, and even a plot to murder Custer, were rumored.

Preparations were made for the execution which was to include that of a criminal and deserter who had been condemned to be shot on the same day.

Custer was told of the ugly mood of his men and his staff asked that they be permitted to carry side-arms to the execution. He refused this request and even one that he alone should carry a sidearm.

His four thousand soldiers formed a hollow square in a nearby field. With considerable alarm, his staff followed as he slowly rode around the entire square close enough to the men that they could reach out and touch him. Following them were the wagons carrying the coffins on which the two condemned men sat. Then came the eight-man firing squad.

The two men were placed before their open graves, their eyes bandaged. All was silence. Quietly, a lone figure under orders, moved up to the sergeant and led him aside. In an instant the command "Fire!" was given, and the deserter fell dead at the side of his waiting grave.

Once the collapsed sergeant was revived, it was explained to him that General Custer thought he had been unduly influenced, and had long decided to pardon him but could not permit the rest of the men to think they had coerced him.

Custer's hand was firm, for lawlessness amongst the troops during that trying period was common enough. The benefits of that firmness was evident on the march to Texas.

The trip to Hempstead, Texas, took most of August, for it was a tedious one of heat and discomfort, yet they traveled but fifteen miles a day. Custer had an ambulance specially fitted for Libbie

PRESIDENTIAL REVIEWING STAND. It was before this stand that Custer's runaway steed, Don Juan, made his wild ride down Pennsylvania Avenue. Courtesy of National Archives.

GENERAL GEORGE A. CUSTER. Painted in New Orleans in July of 1865 just before he was transferred to Texas. Courtesy of J. C. Custer family.

though she rode horseback part of the way. The 4,000 men rode in twos, the wagon and supply train bringing up the rear.

At Hempstead, the Custers were treated with true southern hospitality. Though there was much work to do, for Sheridan had given orders to scour the State for General Kirby Smith's men and arms, there was time for fun. (Smith was a Confederate who refused to turn in his men and arms once he had surrendered.) The planters entertained him by taking him on deer hunts with their well-trained hounds.

Father Custer had joined them, acting as a forage agent for the government. His son Tom and the General plagued him with their practical jokes and he responded each morning by telling them, as his eyes twinkled and he wrinkled his face into a comical smile, what a night of it he had put in. He believed in being a boy with his boys, and they loved him for it.

MRS. GEORGE A. CUSTER. As she appeared while in New Orleans in July of 1865. Painting on a vase. Courtesy of J. C. Custer family.

Lawlessness became widespread in Texas during this period and required a spread of troops over a wide area. At one time the General required thirteen regiments of infantry and as many of cavalry.

Early in the Spring of 1866 Custer was ordered back to Washington to appear before the Joint Committee on Reconstruction, before which he gave testimony as to conditions in Texas and western Louisiana prior to and during military rule. While there he was able to procure a regular army appointment for both his brother Tom and his friend, George Yates.

That same month he was mustered out as a major general of Volunteers, automatically reverting to his regular army rank of captain; his $8,000 a year income dropped accordingly to $2,000. Thus, at the age of 27, he returned to Monroe and a much-earned rest.

Many business opportunities came to him and for awhile he toyed with the appeals of various and enticing propositions to become wealthy. One of the first was an offer of the post of Adjutant General of Mexico with a salary of $16,000 a year in gold. He was highly recommended by both Generals Grant and Sheridan but the question was settled when the Government refused to grant him a year's leave of absence.

PRESIDENT ANDREW JOHNSON. Johnson became president at the death of Abraham Lincoln. He invited Admiral Farragut, and Generals Grant and Custer to join his 1866 campaign junket through the midwest. They all accompanied him. Courtesy of Library of Congress.

In July he received his appointment as Lieutenant-colonel of the newly formed Seventh Cavalry.

Feeling strongly the need to perpetuate a strong constitutional government he took an active part in the National Union Conventions in Philadelphia and Cleveland early that fall. Following this was the "Swing Around The Circle" the Custers made as guests of President Johnson. This trip, though relaxing and pleasant for the two of them, was to bring Custer much criticism from the press.

In early October, while visiting his parents who had moved to Monroe, he answered the query of his old friend General Russell Alger as to his political sentiments. He, among others, had been receiving

TEXAS RECONSTRUCTION HEADQUARTERS. 1. Father Custer. 2. Col. Jacob Greene. 3. Mrs. Custer. 4. Eliza. Tom is seated to immediate left of the General. 1865. Mrs. E. B. Custer collection. Custer Battlefield Museum.

information that Custer had been supporting a Copperhead (any Northerner who had supported the South) for Congress. Custer advised him that his views had not changed about Copperheads; that he still "denounced the men at home who withheld their support from us while in the field." He explained his failure to attack the writers who had attacked him by saying, "The personal spleen which may be indulged in by those who are familiar with paper-bullets will have little effect upon one who has been exposed to bullets of a more deadly character. As I have survived the latter, I certainly need not fear the former."

Late in October Libbie and Autie joined the newly formed Seventh Cavalry at Fort Riley, Kansas.

RECONSTRUCTION HEADQUARTERS. Custer and his cavalry were ordered to Texas in the latter part of 1865 during the turbulent post war period. Custer and his wife are in the center with his brother Tom seated to the immediate left. His father Emanuel is standing at the top right. Mrs. E. B. Custer collection. Custer Battlefield Museum.

SEVENTH CAVALRY REGIMENTAL STANDARD IN 1876. This flag accompanied the regiment to the Battle of the Little Big Horn. It was saved by having been carried by the pack train. Courtesy of Maj. E. S. Luce.

SEVENTH CAVALRY REGIMENTAL STANDARD IN 1951. This flag was carried by the regiment in Japan and Korea. It and the original Standard shown above were displayed on the 75th Anniversary of the Custer Battle. Courtesy of Major E. S. Luce.

GENERAL CUSTER AND MRS. FARNHAM LYON. Out riding near the cavalry camp at Benham, Texas, October 18, 1865. Mrs. E. B. Custer collection. Custer Battlefield Museum.

FIRST LIEUTENANT TOM CUSTER. The General's brother Tom was appointed a first lieutenant in the regular army July 28, 1866. 1867. Courtesy of Custer Battlefield Museum.

Chapter Nine

KANSAS AND COURTMARTIAL

The contrast between the excitement of battle in Virginia and the dull routine of garrison duty was great. Raw recruits, many of whom had never been on a horse, had to be made into cavalrymen. Desertions were commonplace for the food provided was extremely poor and the discipline severe.

The first winter was a trying one for garrison life was extremely confining without the addition of an unusual amount of subzero weather to make it more so. The constant elbow-rubbing of the enlisted men created tensions resulting in frequent outbursts of temper and rebellion at discipline. Drunkenness and lack of a proper *esprit de corps* were Custer's constant problems.

Yet there was time for long rides with Libbie, and for hunting. The latter was participated in by the enlisted men for Custer found that buffalo hunting in particular was invaluable in developing their horsemanship and their ability to shoot.

The beginning of any Indian campaign meant leaving the meager comforts of the garrison. Out on the plains all luxuries, liberties and literature were at an end. The mess would be plain, the discomforts of travel and weather severe. Not one of them could be quoted as saying they desired war with the Indians. All preferred that the Indian Agent handle the Indian problems.

Spring was to bring the beginning of a campaign against the hostile Indians. Many depredations had been committed against the white settlers and travelers and it was because of this situation that four companies of the Seventh Cavalry were ordered out to be met at Fort Riley by General Hancock, then head of the Department of the Missouri, with his artillery and infantry, the last week of March.

The Seventh Cavalry band played "The Girl I Left Behind Me," as they departed for Fort Harker. Nearing Fort Larned the men and horses suffered terribly from the severe cold and a heavy snowstorm. After futilely attempting to arrange a council with the raiding Cheyennes and Sioux, General Hancock ordered an unoccupied Indian village destroyed when he received word from Custer that these same Indians probably had attacked several mail stations on the Smoky Hill stage route, killing, burning and disembowelling some of the white men in them. The next six weeks of Indian fighting amounted to chasing a will-o'-the-wisp for the Indians, once discovered, would be gone before the army scout's report was acted upon by Hancock.

On June first Custer set out from Fort Hays with his cavalry column to scout the area from the Smoky Hill River up to Fort McPherson on the Platte River and, as he states it:

"... thence describe a semicircle to the southward, touching the headwaters of the Republican, and again reach the Platte at or near Fort Sedgwick, at which post we would replenish our supplies; then move directly south to Fort Wallace, on the Smoky Hill, and from there march down the overland route to our starting-point at Fort Hays. This would involve a ride of upwards of one thousand miles."

77

COMPANIONS ON HORSEBACK. General Custer's greatest joy was to swing into the saddle along side of his wife and gallop off onto the Plains. Followed by his orderly and pack of dogs he was soon away from the confines of the post with all its regulations and ceremony. A different Custer emerged, boylike and frolicsome, unmindful of the cares of a few moments before. Sketch by Frederic Remington in *Tenting on the Plains*.

"WELL, YOU ARE A WARM-BLOODED CUSS."

FORT RILEY TO FORT HARKER. The Seventh Cavalry left Fort Riley late in March of 1867. The windswept Kansas prairie was extremely cold at the time. Custer, as usual, paid little attention to the hardships of the trail. Half-frozen General Gibbs could not help notice this characteristic and remark "Well, you are a warm-blooded cuss." Remington sketch in *Tenting on the Plains*.

As Custer's forces neared Fort McPherson on the Republican River, the Indians became more active down on the Smoky Hill. General Sherman met them there with orders to scout the Republican, coming in to Fort Sedgwick for supplies. Meanwhile, Custer had councilled with Pawnee Killer trying to induce him to bring his tribe to Fort McPherson and live their in peace with the whites. This was unsuccessful in spite of Indian promises.

When equidistant from Fort Sedgwick on the north and Fort Wallace on the south, he sent a wagon train to Fort Wallace for supplies. Thinking that Libbie could be reached in time he sent word for her to return with Colonel Cook and the train and remain with him the balance of the summer. However, this message miscarried.

On the morning of June 24th the camp was attacked by Indians, led by Chief Pawnee Killer who had expressed his friendliness for the whites at their council near Fort McPherson. Custer arranged a council in which each side tried to determine the plans of the other, unsuccessfully. An attempt to follow the Indians ended in failure.

The wagon train reached Fort Wallace without incident but on its return was attacked by more than one hundred Indians. Custer's main column moved south to meet Colonel Cook's wagon train.

SEVENTH CAVALRY PETS. Soldiers collect any animal they can pet. The Seventh Cavalry was no exception. Dogs were numerous though hard to keep, Custer frequently owning over a dozen. 1867 sketch by Davis for *Harper's Weekly*.

78

FORT HARKER ENCAMPMENT. This is the site of the beginning of General Winfield S. Hancock's Indian campaign. The Seventh Cavalry camp may be seen at the left. The guidon is to the left of General Custer's tent. The artillery camp is in front. General headquarters is in the middle distance on the right. April 2, 1867. Sketch by Philip D. Fisher in *Harper's Weekly*.

The sharp eyes of the Indians saw the approaching cavalrymen soon after their attack began. It was time to retire.

Shortly after the reunion of the troops, a dispatch was received ordering them to continue their march to Riverside Station west of Fort Sedgwick. Here Custer was surprised to learn that important dispatches had been sent to him from Fort Sedgwick the day following the dispatch he had just received. Ten troopers under command of Lieutenant Kidder and guided by the Sioux chief Red Bead carrying

General Sherman's dispatches had been following his trail. Something had gone wrong.

The supplies being low, the column moved toward Fort Wallace on the following morning. Anxiety as to the fate of Kidder and his men was an impelling factor in the move southward, for there were reports of Indians everywhere.

Desertions had been almost a daily occurrence and had progressed to a point that the command seriously was weakened. The opportunity of obtaining sudden wealth in the mines nearby was a

MEALTIME ON BIG CREEK, KANSAS. General and Mrs. Custer living in the camp style of the period. 1869. Mrs. E. B. Custer collection. Custer Battlefield Museum.

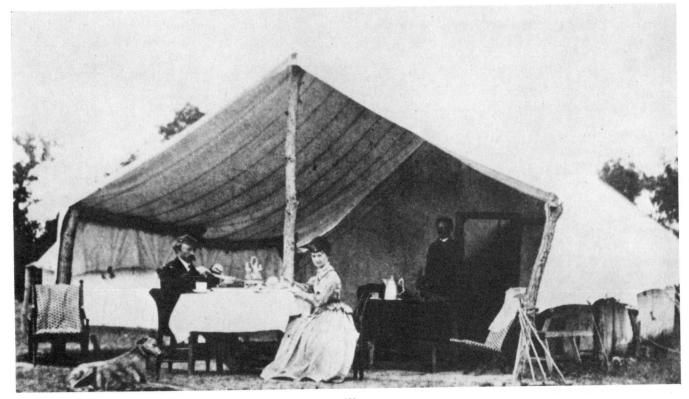

CAMP ON BIG CREEK NEAR FORT HAYS, KANSAS. Tents, left to right: General Custer's tent; Cook's (Eliza) tent; Dining tent; Home tent with sitting room and bedroom. 1869. Author's collection.
Group, left to right: Dr. Dunbar, Mrs. G. A. Custer, Mr. J.R. Young (N.Y. Tribune), Colonel T. B. Weir, Mrs. A. E. Smith, Lt. Colonel G. A. Custer, Mr. Lamborn (Secy. U.P.R.R.), Mrs. Donald McIntosh, Lt. F. M. Gibson.

temptation too great for many of these men. About forty men had deserted during the night before departure. The following noon thirteen more, seven of whom were mounted, deserted in front of the entire regiment. Several officers were ordered to pursue and bring them in, using any measures they thought necessary. One of the deserters raised a gun to fire on his pursuers but promptly was shot down for his efforts along with two of his companions. These with the other three afoot were brought in and the command continued on its way toward Fort Wallace.

Every effort was made to discover the trail of Lieutenant Kidder. On the third day following the desertion episode, Kidder's trail was found stretching toward Fort Wallace, some eighty miles away. Some distance away Scout William Comstock and his Delaware Indians discovered the body of a white horse. Further on was the body of another white horse. There was ample evidence that Kidder's party had been pursued by Indians. Hurrying on they soon came to the site of a terrible battle. Custer wrote:

"Lying in irregular order, and within a very limited circle, were the mangled bodies of poor Kidder and his party, yet so brutally hacked and disfigured as to be beyond recognition save as human beings. Every individual of the party had been scalped and his skull broken— the latter done by some weapon, probably a tomahawk—except the Sioux chief Red Bead, whose scalp had simply been removed from his head and then thrown down by his side."

Each body bristled with from twenty to fifty arrows.

Following burial of the Kidder party, the cavalry column continued on to Fort Wallace, arriving there July thirteenth. It was found that the fort was virtually in a state of siege for the Indians had cut off all supplies and mail along the Smoky Hill for the better part of two weeks. There were daily deaths from cholera and there was little possibility of checking the epidemic without better food and medical supplies.

After several days of rest Custer took about seventy-five of his best-mounted men and set out along the Smoky Hill route with the intent of forcing his way through to Fort Harker, some two hundred miles away, to obtain the needed supplies.

Traveling one hundred and fifty miles in fifty-five hours he arrived at Fort Hays. He left Captain Hamilton at Hays to rest with the command for one day with orders to push on leisurely to Fort Harker while he hurried on to Fort Harker to order supplies and have them ready. Arriving there at two o'clock in the morning, he reported to General A. J. Smith, commander of the military district, and obtained permission to proceed to Fort Riley to see Libbie. He barely had greeted Libbie when he received a telegram from General Smith ordering him to return to his command at once.

On August 27th General Grant ordered a general court martial at Fort Leavenworth trying Custer for: (1) absenting himself from his command near

SEVENTH CAVALRY CAMP ON BIG CREEK. In the spring of 1867 the camp was located some miles from the present city of Hays, Kansas. 1867. Mrs. E. B. Custer collection. Custer Battlefield Museum.

Fort Wallace without authority, (2) using ambulances for personal business, (3) ordering his officers to shoot deserters without the benefit of trial, among other things.

Congress had become quite disturbed over the ineffectiveness of the Hancock campaign, the cost of which had come to about $100,000,000 without having accomplished anything. Congress was demanding an explanation so the army began to look for a scapegoat. Custer did the wrong thing at the right time. Ordinarily his actions would have been overlooked.

The court convened on September 15, 1867, meeting for four weeks, and reaching a verdict of "guilty." He was sentenced *"to be suspended from rank and command for one year and forfeit his pay proper for the same time."* Though it did not appear so at the time, this mandatory vacation was a blessing in disguise.

Not long after the court martial Custer received a call from Judge Kidder, father of Lieutenant Kidder. It was his desire to visit the spot where his son was buried and remove his remains to his home in Dakota territory. It was an exceedingly painful subject for them to discuss, especially when the judge had to be told there was nothing by which any of the bodies positively could be identified. Custer did recall that one retained a collar-band of a checked shirt. He had some cloth of a similar appearance which he showed to the judge, who declared it to be the same kind the lieutenant's mother had used in making him a shirt. In this manner the body was identified and recovered.

General Sheridan had offered his quarters at Fort Leavenworth to the Custers for as long as they wished. Pleasant days followed for they were together again. The time passed rapidly until Spring arrived. Watching the troops prepare for the summer campaign was too much for Autie, so back to Monroe they traveled. Here he spent much time hunting, fishing and writing his memoirs. There were old friends to see and visits to be made in Toledo and Detroit.

The Indian campaign did not do too well that summer. Depredations were increasing in number and severity and the Army seemed unable to do much about it. The climax was reached on September 17, 1868, when nearly nine hundred Sioux and Cheyennes under Roman Nose and Medicine Man attacked General "Sandy" Forsyth and a company of men at Beecher's Island on the Republican River. The defense made by those fifty men is one of the most heroic stories in western history.

While dining at the home of some of his Monroe friends General Custer received a telegram.

Fort Hays, Kansas, September 24, 1868.

General G. A. Custer, Monroe, Michigan

Generals Sherman, Sully, and myself, and nearly all the officers of your regiment, have asked for you, and I hope the applications will be successful. Can you come at once? Eleven companies of your regiment will move about the first of October against the hostile Indians, from Medicine Lodge Creek toward the Wichita Mountains.

P. H. Sheridan, Major General Commanding.

81

FORT McPHERSON, NEBRASKA. As it appeared about the time of the Hancock campaign in 1867. Courtesy of the National Archives.

PRAIRIE CANYON. This was the first sketch to explode the generally accepted idea that Kansas was all prairie. Custer, who may be seen leading this column, had great difficulty in following his campaign course. 1867 sketch by Davis for *Harper's Weekly*.

SIOUX ATTEMPT AT STAMPEDE. The cavalry had to maintain a constant guard to prevent the Indians from driving off their horses. In the instance depicted nearly 200 Indians attempted to drive off the Seventh Cavalry horses. Obtaining them meant great wealth to the Indians. Losing them meant slow, grueling marches to the cavalrymen. 1867 sketch by Davis in *Harper's Weekly*.

INDIANS ATTACKING A WAGON TRAIN. Seventh Cavalry supply wagons were placed in two columns with the lead horses between while the men formed a circle around them to ward off the Sioux and Cheyenne circling attack. Sketch in *Life On The Plains*.

CUSTER'S CONFERENCE WITH PAWNEE KILLER. The Sioux Indian chief "Pawnee Killer" was destined to give Custer repeated trouble. Here he is shown, after his first skirmish with Custer, in a conference he had the impudence to ask for. He demanded coffee, sugar, and ammunition, while he used the opportunity to observe the strength of Custer's regiment. 1867 sketch by Davis for *Harper's Weekly*.

SIOUX ATTACK ON SEVENTH CAVALRY. A view of the disposition of the troopers when attacked by superior numbers near the forks of the Republican River.

Indians frequently attack any sizeable force by circling around it, keeping their horses in constant motion. They have the advantage of being difficult to hit while their prey remain stationary targets. In this instance every third trooper is the horseholder for his own and two other horses, for a stampede of their mounts would leave them practically helpless. 1867 sketch by Davis for *Harper's Weekly*.

BURNING THE CHEYENNE VILLAGE. General Hancock burned this Cheyenne Indian village after he had learned that they had killed some guards and stationmasters on the Smoky Hill stage route. This was the beginning of the Hancock campaign of 1867, that was to end in General Custer's courtmartial. April 19, 1867 sketch by Theodore R. Davis for *Harper's Weekly*.

KIDDER MASSACRE. One of the front page stories of 1867 was the discovery of the bodies of Lieutenant Kidder and his ten men by General Custer. Kidder had been detailed to carry a message to Custer from General Sherman. He and his party were attacked by "Pawnee Killer" and horribly mutilated. 1867 sketch by Davis for *Harper's Weekly*.

84

FORT WALLACE, KANSAS. View of the officers quarters in 1865. Today neither a board nor a brick exists at the site of the once famous post. The Fort Wallace Memorial Association has a plan for its reconstruction. From an 1865 postcard view.

GENERAL CUSTER'S SCOUTS. Left to right—Custer's chief of scouts, Will Comstock, was said to be the best interpreter on the plains.

Ed Guerrier, a halfbreed Cheyenne, had little use for Indians, consequently lived, talked and dressed as a whiteman.

Thomas Atkins. once was employed by the freighters, Russell, Majors & Waddell. An extremely brave man, he was one of the best couriers in the Indian country.

Kincade was a courier too. Couriers usually traveled their dangerous missions at night for the Indians were less watchful then. Few frontiersmen would take this dangerous job of message carrying. 1867 sketch by Davis for *Harper's Weekly.*

SMOKING THE PEACEPIPE. Custer used every opportunity to hold council with the Indians so he could study and influence them. This occasion occurred near Pawnee Fork, Kansas in the Spring of 1867. Sketch by Remington in *Tenting on the Plains*.

CUSTER'S QUARTERS AT FORT RILEY, KANSAS. The house remains in constant use to this day apparently retaining its original plumbing. It is number 24 Sheridan Ave. Courtesy of the Army General School, 1953.

MAJOR GENERAL PHILIP SHERIDAN. After Custer was court-martialed and sentenced Sheridan offered him the use of his Fort Leavenworth apartment for as long as he liked. Brady photo courtesy of Ansco.

CALIFORNIA JOE. Moses Embree Milner was appointed chief of scouts for the Washita campaign. He got drunk the very first night and was immediately relieved of his job as chief. As a scout thereafter he was extremely valuable. He was rarely seen without his pipe, his gun or his dog, and usually rode his favorite mule. Courtesy of National Archives.

Chapter Ten

RETURN TO THE PLAINS

Custer arrived at Fort Hays, Kansas, on the morning of September 30th. At breakfast General Sheridan told him, "Custer, I rely on you in everything, and shall send you on this expedition without orders, leaving you to act entirely on your own judgment."

On the afternoon that he rejoined his regiment it was attacked by a band of Indians. He soon learned that this had been a daily occurrence and that the camp had been reduced into almost a state of siege. The men, though untrained and unfamiliar with Indian warfare, were rapidly becoming acquainted with their guns and horses through these daily sorties.

To catch the fleet Indian ponies with the aid of the more ponderous domestic horses of the cavalry was impossible. To follow them was equally difficult for the ponies could maintain their strength on the grass of the plains, while grain and forage had to be carried for the cavalry horses. It was decided, at Custer's suggestion, that the best time for a campaign would be in the winter when the ponies were weakest and while the entire tribe was congregated along some stream. In doing so they were following that maxim of war that decreed one should do what the enemy does not expect. ·

For the first time the Seventh Cavalry was to serve as one body. All horses were newly shod and many fresh horses were substituted. There was a "coloring of the horses" whereby each company was to have horses of one color. Once this had been completed daily target practice was ordered for all. As an incentive it was announced that out of the eight hundred men the forty best marksmen would be made into a corps of sharpshooters to march as a unit and to be exempt from guard duty.

It was determined that many of the depredating tribes camped in the winter along the Washita River. This was due south of Fort Hays, in Oklahoma, just east of the Texas Panhandle. Bases of supply would lie between Fort Dodge below Fort Hays and at Camp Supply further to the south.

The column left Camp Supply November 23rd during a raging snowstorm and with more than a foot of snow on the ground. Custer planned to find the winter hiding place of the hostile Indians and to administer such punishment as he was able. Though uncomfortable for the men in the cavalry column the snow prevented the Indian villages from moving and lulled the redskins into a sense of security.

The wagon train, eleven companies of cavalry numbering nearly nine hundred men, and the detachment of scouts headed by *California Joe* and a delegation of friendly Osage Indians headed

DUEL. The Cheyennes and the troopers soon paired off and fought it out. By Schreyvogel. Mrs. E. B. Custer collection. Custer Battlefield Museum.

MY BUNKIE. Both the Indian and the trooper takes care of their own. By Schreyvogel. Mrs. E. B. Custer collection. Custer Battlefield Museum.

by chiefs *Little Beaver* and *Hard Rope* traveled fifteen miles the first day. Visibility was so poor that Custer had to use a compass to guide the column to its first night encampment on Wolf Creek.

On the fourth day out Major Elliot, while scouting the north bank of the Canadian River, discovered the trail of a war party of one hundred and fifty Indians. When informed, Custer ordered Elliot in pursuit while he detailed eighty men to accompany the wagon train. The rest of the troopers were to carry with them one hundred rounds of ammunition each in addition to small amounts of coffee, hard bread, and forage for their horses. It was Custer's design to move in a direction so as to strike Elliot's trail. Scout Corbin was detailed to inform Elliot accordingly. The troopers struggled on until 9 o'clock that night before arriving at the point that Elliot and his three troops had stopped. While resting briefly the Osages were counciled and all were of the opinion that the Indian villages were not far away. All strongly advised that the

pursuit be discontinued until daylight. This, Custer concluded, was the natural reluctance of the Indian to attack an unseen foe.

Orders were given to discontinue all bugle calls and the column moved on at 10 p.m., the two Osage guides leading the way some three or four hundred yards in advance, and the cavalry about a quarter of a mile in the rear. Orders were given prohibiting speech above a whisper. No one was permitted to light a match. Soon the embers of a dying fire were discovered; then a dog was heard to bark, followed by the tinkling of a bell in a pony herd.

Though past midnight, the command was divided into four equal parts and so positioned as to completely surround the village and attack it at daylight. In the four-hour interval it grew intensely cold. The men were not permitted even to stamp their feet to keep warm.

Suddenly there was a shot on the far side of the

BATTLE OF THE WASHITA. The attack was a complete surprise. From a sketch in *My Life On The Plains.*

RETURN FROM THE WASHITA. The return to Camp Supply was a happy event for the weatherbeaten troopers. From *My Life On The Plains.*

WASHITA. The Seventh Cavalry attacked the Indian village on the Washita River on dawn of November 27, 1868. Painting by James E. Taylor. Mrs. E. B. Custer collection. Custer Battlefield Museum.

FALLEN FOE. No quarter was shown the enemy on either side for no mercy was expected. By Schreyvogel. Mrs. E. B. Custer collection. Custer Battlefield Museum.

village. Custer ordered the band to begin and immediately were heard the stirring notes of the Seventh's famous fighting song "Garry Owen." From all sides came the cheers of the men and the calls of the trumpeters. The Battle of the Washita had begun. The Indians quickly overcame their surprise and began a vigorous defense. Some fired from behind the nearest trees while others sprang into the waist-deep water of the Washita using its banks as a protection from the well-directed fire of the troopers. Squaws and boys in their early teens took arms against their foe. Major Benteen was fired upon three times by one of these teenage boys and, after his own horse had been wounded was forced to kill the boy to avoid being killed by him.

In one instance, a squaw leading a small white boy was intercepted by several troopers. When she observed that her escape had been cut off she drew a knife from her blanket and plunged it into the

nearly-naked body of her unknown captive. She was quickly dispatched.

So desperate was the village defense that seventeen warriors occupying a depression in the ground could not be driven from their position. After a number of troopers had been shot down sharpshooters were employed to annihilate them. In a nearby ravine the bodies of thirty-eight warriors were counted.

By 10 a.m. the fight was still in progress when a small group of Indians was observed on a knoll about a mile below the village. On inquiry from one of the captured squaws Custer was surprised to learn that they were from a series of villages extending for ten miles along the Washita and comprised of Cheyennes, Kiowas, Comanches, Arapahoes, and some Apaches. As the numbers increased there was no uncertainty in his mind that he shortly was to be attacked by superior numbers. It was time to survey the situation.

RUNNING FIGHT. Much of the Washita fight was in the saddle. By Schreyvogel. Mrs. E. B. Custer collection. Custer Battlefield Museum.

ATTACK AT DAWN. Custer's dawn attack on the Washita was a tactic borrowed from the Indians. By Charles Schreyvogel. Mrs. E. B. Custer collection. Custer Battlefield Museum.

The Indians increased in numbers on all sides keeping up a continuous fire. Though completely surrounded, the soldiers fought valiantly; suddenly quartermaster Major Bell with an escort arrived with a much-needed supply of ammunition. The order was given to tear down and burn the lodges and the huge piles of captured property. Since it was impossible to take the ponies with them, and to turn them loose would provide the Indians with a means of attack and pursuit, Custer ordered all shot.

A search was made for Major Elliot and his nineteen men over an area of two miles and finally it was concluded they had been lost. It was now about an hour before nightfall, and the safety of the supply train as well as of the men was of great concern.

It was then that Custer demonstrated his tactical ability. With the band playing and guidons waving, the entire regiment with a strong force of skirmishers in advance set out down the valley toward the remaining villages. Momentarily the Indian spectators on the surrounding hills were silent. Then, as if discerning that the troops intended continuing their destruction on the occupants of the other villages, they hastened ahead of the troops without firing a shot. This latter course probably was followed so that Custer's Indian hostages would not be injured by stray bullets.

GENERAL CUSTER AT THE WASHITA. This was Custer's dress for the Washita Campaign. Over this he wore the buffalo coat that may be seen in the Monroe Museum. Mrs. E. B. Custer collection. Custer Battlefield Museum.

At the beginning of the attack Capt. Louis McLane Hamilton had been killed. Captain Barnitz had been wounded near the heart, apparently mortally. Tom Custer and another officer had been shot while nineteen enlisted men had been killed and eleven wounded. Fifty-three squaws and children had been captured along with 875 ponies, 1,100 buffalo robes, 500 pounds of powder, 1,000 pounds of lead, 4,000 arrows, and immense quantities of stored foods and equipment. Of the warriors under Satanta, Little Raven and Black Kettle, one hundred and three had been killed including the Chief, Black Kettle. Of Major Elliot and his detachment nothing had been seen since they followed a group of retreating Indians early in the day.

MAJOR JOEL H. ELLIOTT. Major Elliott, leading 15 enlisted men, was ambushed and killed. Their absence was discovered after the battle was over when the pressure of the Indians from surrounding villages made it unwise to recover their bodies. Courtesy of Custer Battlefield Museum.

Long after dark the first deserted village was reached, whereupon Custer countermarched his men toward the battleground, arriving there about ten o'clock. Without halting he pushed on following the trail he had made the night before. The brisk march was continued until 2 o'clock in the morning and then they went into bivouac, a squadron having been sent forward to meet the supply train. At daylight they were back in the saddle, and at 10 a.m. they had the great satisfaction of meeting the train. California Joe immediately was sent with a dispatch to General Sheridan. He took the scout Jack Corbin with him, the two of them accomplishing the errand through enemy-ridden country at night in record time.

On December 2nd, a mild winter day, the command began its last day's march toward Camp Supply. General Sheridan was advised by courier of the hour in the forenoon that the column would arrive at his headquarters and that it would be their pleasure to march in review before him and his staff.

The day was bright and the ground in excellent shape as it led in a long gradual slope into the valley. The Osage guides and trailers, dressed and painted, led the column, chanting their war songs and at intervals giving their war-whoops or firing their guns in the air. Next came the scouts with California Joe astride his mule. Following them were the Indian prisoners under guard, all mounted, and dressed in bright colors which was quite a contrast to the colorless clothing of the scouts ahead. Then came the band playing "Garry Owen," followed by the troops in platoons, the leading one

LIEUTENANT TOM CUSTER. Brother Tom was slightly wounded at the Washita. Mrs. E. B. Custer collection. Custer Battlefield Museum.

AUTIE, LIBBIE AND TOM. In camp near Big Creek, 1869. Mrs. E. B. Custer collection. Custer Battlefield Museum.

FRIENDLY INDIAN? Attired in beaver furs and a bearclaw necklace, his purpose is peace. Mrs. E. B. Custer collection. Custer Battlefield Museum.

FOE? War bonnet and war hatchet usually indicate war. Mrs. E. B. Custer collection. Custer Battlefield Museum.

being that of Colonel Cook's sharpshooters. As the officers gave General Sheridan the sabre salute he returned it by lifting his cap. The look of pride on his face was the greatest reward he could have given them. He later stated that the scene was the most beautiful and highly interesting he had ever witnessed.

As Custer had predicted, the campaign would produce criticism no matter how it ended. Had they failed to find and defeat the Indians, those who had been victims of their assaults would have made extremely uncomplimentary remarks as to military efficiency and energy. As it resulted, many well-intentioned people throughout the country were distressed over the measures taken against the depredators. One group of traders and Indian agents, though well informed, charged that the Indians attacked were friendly and peaceable. They were loud in expressing their pseudo-horror for they were growing rich off the Indians' economic ignorance. Yet they knew well enough that the Indians attacked had been guilty of repeated depredations and had been caught with the evidence—white prisoners.

WASHITA PRISONERS. The 53 prisoners were squaws and children. Rarely is a warrior taken alive. Mute testimony to this are the 103 warriors who died in the battle. Mrs. E. B. Custer collection. Custer Battlefield Museum.

SEVENTH CAVALRY CAPTIVES. The scout at the left stands with a group of Washita captives at Fort Dodge, Kansas. Mrs. E. B. Custer collection. Custer Battlefield Museum.

CHEYENNES. Taken in the Washita valley. Mrs. E. B. Custer collection. Custer Battle Museum.

EVENING PARADE. Seventh Cavalry in 1869 near Fort Hays. Mrs. E. B. Custer collection. Custer Battlefield Museum.

FORT HAYS, KANSAS. Camp of the Seventh Cavalry near Big Creek while guarding the construction crew of the Kansas Pacific Railroad during 1869. Mrs. E. B. Custer collection. Custer Battlefield Museum.

MULE RACE. Evidence of the cavalryman's sense of humor and sporting blood. Author's collection.

UNITED STATES COURSE

Fort Leavenworth, Kansas.

JUNE MEETING,

TUESDAY, JUNE 16th, 1868, 4 P. M.

MULE RACE!

OFFICERS' PURSE: - - - $50.

ONE MILE DASH - SLOW RACE.

1. General Custer enters **HYANKEDANK**, by **Hifalutin**, out of **Snollygoster**, second dam **Buckjump**, by **Thunder**, out of **You Bet**.
Age, three score years and ten. Colors, ring-ed, streak-ed and strip-ed.

2. General McKeever enters **HARD TACK**, by **Commissary**, by **Eaton**, (eatin',) second dam **Contractor**, by **Morgan**, out of **Missouri**.
Age, forty years Colors, Purple, tipped with Orange.

3. Colonel Parsons enters **SYMMETRY**, (see me try,) by **Considerably**, out of **Pocket**, second dam **Polly Tix**, by **Nasby**, out of **Office**.
Age, seventeen years, Colors, Uncommonly-Blue.

4. Captain Yates enters **WILLIAM TELL**, by **Switzerland**, by **Apple Tree**, second dam **Gessler**, by **Hapsburg**, out of **Austria**.
Age, eighteen years. Colors, Apple-Green.

5. Lieutenant Leary enters **TRUMP**, by **Card**, out of **Contractor**, second dam **Leader**, by **Mule-Teer**, out of **Wagon**.
Age, ten years. Colors, Lemon.

6. Lieutenant Jackson enters **ABYSSINIA**, by **Napier**, out of **Africa**, dam **Theodorus**, by **Solomon**, out of **Magdala**.
Age, thirty-nine years. Colors, Scarlet, Yellow Spots.

7. Colonel Myers enters **PIZZARRO**, by **Peru**, out of **South America**, second dam **Cuzco**, by **Incas**, out of **Andes**.
Age, sixteen years. Colors, Light Brown.

8. Lieutenant Umbstaetter enters **SKIRMISHER**, by **Picket**, out of **Camp**, second dam **Carbine**, by **Breech Loader**, out of **Magazine**.
Age, twenty-five years. Colors, Dark Blue, tipped with Red.

9. Lieutenant Moylan enters **BREAK-NECK**, by **Runaway**, out of **Would'nt Go**, second dam **Contusion** by **Collision**, out of **Accident**.
Age, fifty-six. Colors, Sky Blue.

10. Captain Huntington, enters **SPAVIN**, by **Quartermaster**, out of **Government**, second dam (not worth one.)
Age, twenty-one years. Colors, A-Knock-to-Ruin. (An Octaroon.)

11. Lieutenant Howe, enters **SLOW** by **Tardy**, out of **Late**, second dam **Lazy**, by **Inactive**.
Age, three times 6, four times seven, twenty-eight and 11. Colors, Queer.

12. Lieutenant Dunwoody, enters **HORATIO**, by **Dexterity**, by **Taunt**, second dam **Estop**,
Age, fourteen years. Colors, Tawney.

13. Captain Weir enters **REVOLUTIONIST**, by **Hard Luck**, out of **Rib Smasher**, second dam **Blood Blister**, by **Can't-Stand-it**, out of **Let's Quit**.
Age, sixteen, Colors, Black-and-Blue,

Note.—THE MONEY ACCRUING FROM THIS RACE IS TO BE DEVOTED TO THE SUPPORT OF THE WIDOWS AND ORPHANS MADE SO THEREBY.

SOLDIER'S FAMILY. A scene at Fort Hays about 1869. Mrs. E. B. Custer collection. Custer Battlefield Museum.

Chapter Eleven

WARPAINT TO PEACE

This was only the beginning. General Sheridan in his congratulatory message to the Seventh Cavalry referred to the Battle of the Washita as "the opening of the campaign against hostile Indians south of Arkansas." There was to be no let up. Friendly Indians were to return to their reservations for they could only be determined by the land on which they resided.

All Indian agents were advised to order their "friendlies" to do so since soldiers could not tell good Indians from bad by the clothes they wore. It was vital that they do so for Sheridan wanted all warring Indians punished and he considered all Indians off their reservation as such.

The people of Kansas had been aroused by the Indian murders of men, women and children, the burning of houses, the running off of vast amounts of stock, and the carrying off into captivity of a number of women. The governor had obtained federal permission to raise a regiment of cavalry to act in liaison with the federal troops. It was this Nineteenth Kansas Cavalry, all Kansas volunteers under the command of Colonel S. J. Crawford, the state's former governor, that reached Camp Supply in time to join General Custer in the next campaign.

Leaving for the battleground of the Washita on December 7th, General Sheridan accompanied them, for it was his desire to determine the fate of Major Elliot and his party. With little difficulty they came upon the horribly mutilated bodies of the men. It was evident that Elliot, seeing the hopelessness of breaking through the lines, had ordered his men to dismount and put up a defensive action. They were found in a circle twenty yards in diameter, the empty shells near each giving ample evidence of a determined defense.

The valley was a scene of disorder and abandonment some ten miles in length with evidences that there had been more than six hundred lodges there during the battle. In the deserted camp of Satanta's Kiowas were discovered the bodies of a young white woman and a child violently murdered.

Following the trail leading from the villages for the next seven days the Osage scouts galloped in on the morning of December 17th and reported a party of Indians bearing a flag of truce. With them was another scout from Fort Cobb bearing a message from General Hazen, a reputable Indian agent, stating that all Indians between Fort Cobb and Custer's troopers were friendly and had not been on the warpath that season. The same scout bearing the dispatch informed Custer that another scout accompanying him had been seized as a prisoner of war by Satanta and Lone Wolf just a mile back. These were the same Indians approaching under a flag of truce.

98

SATANTA. A Kiowa chief who, with "Lone Wolf," was held as hostage by Custer.
Courtesy of the National Archives.

LONE WOLF. A Kiowa chief.
Courtesy of the National Archives.

its volunteered accompaniment to Fort Cobb, Custer ordered them made prisoners. It was only after a period of imprisonment at Fort Cobb, during which time both chiefs used various strategems to obtain release, that Sheridan finally ordered them hanged by a specified time if their tribesmen did not come into the reservation. The Indians complied with his demand.

Couriers were sent to two hostile villages that had refused to come in, the Arapahoes and the Cheyennes, but with no positive results. Custer finally approached General Sheridan with the suggestion that he be permitted to take forty men and seek the tribes with the purpose of convincing their chiefs of the friendly desire of the government. If he took a large force it might be interpreted as meaning war; if he were to take too small a force it would tempt the Indians to murder them. Sheridan said he would not order Custer to do this but would allow him if he volunteered. Taking most of his men from the sharpshooters, and including his brother Tom, Captain Robbins, Dr. Renick, Neva, Little Robe, Yellow Bear, and Romero, he set out.

They soon reached the village of the Arapahoes and convinced them of the value of returning to the reservation. Search for the Cheyennes was unsuccessful and the men returned to camp for a rest and replenishment of supplies.

Custer quickly noted they all were painted for war and were well armed. They obviously would have attacked had they not seen a larger force than their own. These were the same Kiowas in whose camp had been found the bodies of a slain white woman and child and yet they presented Custer with a certificate of good behavior dated just the day before. Following the meeting, at which the chiefs agreed to release the captured scout, they asked to accompany the command to Fort Cobb, along with their camp. Some eighteen or twenty stayed with the soldiers but on one pretext or another in the next few days dwindled down until only head chiefs Satanta and Lone Wolf remained. Sensing that all of this was to divert attention from the village, which had already strayed away from

LITTLE RAVEN. A chief of the Arapahoes, he was peacefully inclined as the result of a conference with Custer. Courtesy of the National Archives.

As soon as arrangments could be made, Custer faced his command westward, passing along the southern base of the Wichita Mountains in search of the Cheyennes. A trail was struck running westward, which was followed as close as could be done prudently. A rain began to fall the next day and then the Osage scouts discovered an Indian camp a short distance ahead. Approaching the camp by stealth, it was discovered to have been abandoned, and in such haste that pack animals and ponies had been left behind. It later developed that the Indians had discovered the presence of the troops through the barking of several dogs traveling with the command.

The march was resumed but there was no trail to follow for the Indians had vanished as if into thin air. An old trail of a single lodge (tepee) was discovered and it was decided to follow its southwesterly direction. Late in the day it was found to join a number of others and it was the opinion of

CAPTAIN FREDERICK W. BENTEEN. An original member of the Seventh Cavalry, he was a bitter enemy of Custer. Photo by G. G. Griers. Courtesy of the Custer Battlefield Museum.

the scouts that the Indians had used it just two weeks before.

Cautiously following the trail, and covering in one day what had taken the Indians three, a camp site soon was reached of some four hundred lodges that had been occupied the day previous. The Osages kept well in advance and soon were able to report the presence of an encampment a mile to their front. Anxious to identify the tribe, though quite sure they were the Cheyennes that held two white girls captive, Custer made signals to them for a conference. He knew that if a shot was fired from either side it would be the signal for the murder of the girls. He was approached by several Cheyennes and conducted to the village where he was able to determine positively that the white girls were there.

Fifty or more chiefs and warriors accompanied

CAPTAIN THOMAS B. WEIR. A survivor of the Battle of the Little Big Horn. Author's collection.

him back to his camp and proceeded to entertain him with Indian music and superb exhibitions of horsemanship. Aware that something was afoot he placed sentries in positions of observation. He soon was rewarded for reports came in that the village was preparing to decamp. Ordering his officers to quietly leave and return with one hundred well-armed men, one at a time, so as not to excite suspicion, he awaited the time they all had returned, then told his interpreter Romero to inform the Indians he had something of importance to convey to them.

Custer unbuckled his revolver and threw it on the ground as evidence that he desired no bloodshed, asking the chiefs to look around and count the armed soldiers. Then telling them that he had observed their purpose and now had them in his power it would be better that they offer no resistance. There was an immediate exit of all the warriors except four chiefs, these four being the ones he desired to retain. He explained to them that they were prisoners but that they could chose one of their number who would be sent to their village with his demands.

CAPTAIN MYLES MOYLAN. A survivor of the Battle of the Little Big Horn. Author's collection.

WHERE MAJOR ELLIOTT FELL. X—in the foreground indicates where Major Elliott fell. Trees in the background line the banks of the Washita River. The arrow marks a butte immediately above the main battlefield. Mrs. E. B. Custer collection. Custer Battlefield Museum.

Custer wrote in *My Life on the Plains*,

> I accordingly caused bountiful presents of coffee and sugar to be given the one so chosen, returned to him his pony and arms, and entrusted him with verbal messages to his tribe, the substance of which was as follows: First, I demanded the unconditional surrender of the two white girls held captive in the village; hitherto surrenders of white captives by Indians had only been made on payment of heavy ransom. Secondly, I required the Cheyenne village, as an evidence of peaceable intentions and good faith on their part, to proceed at once to their reservation. . . . Thirdly, I sent a friendly message to Little Robe, inviting him to visit me with a view to speedy settlement of the questions at issue. . . .

Various subterfuges were resorted to by the Cheyennes during the next few days in avoiding the surrender of the white girls. Finally Custer sent for the chiefs of the Cheyenne village to issue an ultimatum. When they arrived he recounted the incidents of the last few days, and after drawing attention to the weakness of their ponies he ended by giving them until sunset of the following day to return the white girls or the three chiefs he held would forfeit their lives.

WASHITA MONUMENT. Monument indicates the location of the battlefield on the Washita River. Photo by W. S. Scott, 1890. Mrs. E. B. Custer collection. Custer Battlefield Museum.

BLACK KETTLE TREE. The space in the foreground was occupied by the Cheyenne lodges when they were attacked by Custer's troopers November 27, 1868. Photo by W. S. Scott, 1890. Mrs. E. B. Custer collection. Custer Battlefield Museum.

OSAGE SCOUTS AND INTERPRETERS. Custer's "eyes and ears" in the Washita campaign. 1868. Mrs. E. B. Custer collection. Custer Battlefield Museum.

CUSTER'S PARLEY. General Custer demands that "Lone Wolf" and "Satanta" brings their Kiowa tribes onto their reservation at Fort Cobb. By Shreyvogel. Mrs. E. B. Custer collection. Custer Battlefield Museum.

The next day passed with no sign of movement from the direction of the village. One hour before sunset twenty mounted figures could be seen to the west. As they approached it became apparent that two of the group were the girls in question.

Since the Kansas volunteer cavalry had sacrificed so much to effect a release of the girls, Custer designated them as the ones to first welcome them back to civilization. Clothed as they were in dresses made of flour sacks, leggins and moccasins, and with their hair in long braids, they gave every evidence of deprivation and suffering. Exchanged from chief to chief they had been subjected to every indignity one could imagine. Beaten by

CUSTER AND HIS SCOUTS. Custer stands in front of his tent near Fort Dodge. His Osage Indian scouts are seated in front of him. His pet pelican stands in front of the guidon. 1868. Mrs. E. B. Custer collection. Custer Battlefield Museum.

WASHITA SCOUTS. X—indicates Captain Hale of the infantry. The others are Custer's scouts, and some citizens of Fort Cobb. Mrs. E. B. Custer collection. Custer Battlefield Museum.

squaws, starved and half frozen, their joy at regaining freedom after a year of captivity well can be imagined.

Once the girls had been returned, a delegation from the village asked for the chiefs' release, but were told that there was another condition of the agreement to be met. Seeing there would be no modification in the agreement, the Indians slowly moved their village into Camp Supply and surrendered.

When General Sheridan received a detailed account of the operations he sent a letter of congratulations for the success of the winter's campaign. The Kansas volunteers marched to Fort Hays to be mustered out, for they had accomplished the purpose for which they had volunteered, while the Seventh Cavalry was ordered there for a much deserved rest. For once all was quiet on the Kansas plains.

CALL ON THE COMMANDING OFFICER. An officer who had been out on a campaign was frequently kidded into thinking that the new commanding officer was a stickler for proper dress.

HOSTAGES. Cheyenne chiefs "Fat Bear," "Big Head," and "Dull Knife" were the hostages seized by Custer to compel the release of two white women they held captive. After threatening to hang the chiefs, the women were freed. Mrs. E. B. Custer collection. Custer Battlefield Museum.

PEACE COMMISSION IN 1868. At Fort Laramie, on April 29, 1868, a peace commission met with the Sioux and signed an agreement to abandon Forts Phil Kearney, C. F. Smith and Reno.

Left to right: Gen. A. H. Terry, Gen. W. S. Harney, Gen. W. T. Sherman, a Sioux squaw, Indian Commissioner N. G. Taylor, S. F. Tappan and Gen. C. C. Augur. Courtesy of the National Archives.

CUSTER NEAR FORT DODGE. The General is shown with three of his greyhounds and his pet pelican. 1868. Mrs. E. B. Custer collection. Custer Battlefield Museum.

Chapter Twelve

RAILROADS MUST MOVE WEST

The Summer of 1869 offered its compensations for the hardships of the previous Winter. Though garrison duty eventually became dull, for the moment it provided the thrill of the hunt and the many happy moments of reunion with Libbie. A string of visitors from the East and from Europe began to arrive, attracted by Custer's fame as an Indian fighter. In October the Custers moved to Fort Leavenworth where he again resumed his writing. In the latter part of the year he traveled east, spending part of the time in Monroe to help clear up some of the problems of Judge Bacon's estate.

Spring saw them at Fort Hays again for the Seventh Cavalry must patrol the plains. Occasionally small parties of Indians would leave their reservations and indulge in cattle stealing. These non-conformists had to be apprehended and herded back onto their own lands.

The summer of 1870 brought an increase in the number of visitors and notables. Many came for the express purpose of going on a buffalo hunt and Custer, genial host that he was, saw to it that each request was properly filled. There was so little to do now that the Indian problem had been settled that other regiments were asking for duty at this post. Rumors of an assignment of the Seventh Cavalry to another area were so well founded that Custer made a trip to Washington to try to spike the transfer.

In March of 1871, part of the Seventh was assigned to South Carolina for the purpose of breaking up the Ku Klux Klan, and to hunt down illegal distillers. The balance of the regiment under Custer was sent to Elizabethtown, Kentucky, for two years of routine duty. Part of his time here was spent in Louisville buying horses for the regiment, a procedure which eventually led him into the purchasing of racehorses as a personal investment.

In January of 1872, Autie was ordered to accompany General Sheridan on a buffalo hunt given by the government for the purpose of entertaining the Grand Duke Alexis of Russia and his ducal party. At that time buffalo hunting was the most famous sport in America. Since Alexis was the representative of a friendly country and a son of its czar, it was thought advisable to entertain him with this most exciting of sports.

Every effort was exerted to make this a memorable occasion for the duke. Generals Ord, Switzer, Palmer, Forsyth and Custer were placed in charge of arrangements. Chief Spotted Tail and about one hundred of his Sioux chiefs and warriors were asked to put on a dance and to give an exhibition of their method of hunting buffalo. Buffalo Bill Cody was retained as one of the guides. A

107

DANDY AND VIC. On the left is Custer's favorite hunting mount, "Dandy," held by his orderly Private John Burkman. On the right is "Vic," the horse Custer rode in his last battle. Vic was not killed but was acquired by one of the victorious Sioux. Some of the General's hunting dogs may be seen. Courtesy of Custer Battlefield Museum.

number of officers accompanied by two companies of cavalry and the Second Cavalry Band escorted the ducal party from the railroad station on the North Platte River over to Camp Alexis on Red Willow Creek, Nebraska.

General Custer and Buffalo Bill appeared in their frontier buckskin hunting outfits which, at a distance, gave them the appearance of Indians. The hunt started on the morning of January 14th and after several days of excellent hunting, entertaining

Indian war dances and bow and arrow hunting exhibitions, the party moved on to Denver and Topeka, stopping at Forts Wallace and Hays on the way. Custer was a constant companion of the Grand Duke for they had taken an instantaneous liking to each other at the first meeting.

Moving on to St. Louis, then Louisville, the party was lavishly entertained at every point. Through the Grand Duke's insistence Custer was permitted to accompany the party to New Orleans where it boarded the waiting Russian Fleet. Then Custer returned to Elizabethtown.

In March, 1873, the Seventh Cavalry again was ordered to the plains. Reunited at Memphis, the regiment traveled by boat and then train to Yankton, Dakota Territory. Custer celebrated this order to move, as he had every previous order, with wild demonstrations of joy. Mrs. Custer writes in *Boots and Saddles* of his throwing a chair out into the kitchen and, "as for me I was tossed about the room, and all sorts of jokes were played upon me before the frolic ended. After such participation in the celebration, I was almost too tired with the laughter and fun to begin packing."

LEUTENANT GENERAL P. H. SHERIDAN AND STAFF. Left to right: Gen. G. A. Custer, Col. G. A. Forsyth, Lieut. Gen. P. H. Sheridan, Maj. M. V. Asche, Gen. N. B. Sweitzer. Col. M. V. Sheridan, Gen. J. W. Forsyth. Taken in Topeka, Kansas in 1872. Courtesy of Custer Battlefield Museum.

She added that, "This removal to Dakota meant to my husband a reunion with his regiment and summer campaigns against the Indians; to me it meant months of loneliness, anxiety and terror."

The contrast between the weather in Memphis and in Yankton was great, and was exaggerated further by a great blizzard in which the only shelter was a shack. Several cavalrymen lost feet and fingers but no one died.

One week later the column started on the five hundred mile ride to Fort Rice. Barely traveling four miles an hour the column reached Fort Rice six weary weeks later; a steamer carried them on to Bismarck. Once at Bismarck, Libbie, with the general's sister, Margaret Calhoun, took the train for Monroe, for the regiment had been ordered into the field to protect the surveyors of the Northern Pacific Railway.

Colonel D. S. Stanley was to command the escort of more than 1,500 officers and men which consisted of 20 companies of infantry, and 10 companies of cavalry under its Lieutenant Colonel, George Armstrong Custer. There would be 275 wagons and ambulances carrying sufficient rations and forage to last 60 days. One of the problems

LIEUTENANT HENRY J. NOWLAN. One of the officers in the Battle of the Washita. Custer Battlefield Museum.

was to decide on the amount of forage to carry for the 2,321 horses and mules, since the daily mileage of the engineers was unknown.

Action was the sort of thing Custer lived for, and preparing for it made the days pass rapidly. Adding to the joy of the occasion was the discovery that the chief of the Northern Pacific's engineers was his old West Point classmate and friend, the Confederate General Thomas L. Rosser. There

CAVALRY AND INFANTRY OFFICERS CONVERSE. Left to right: Lieutenant Charles Varnum, Lieutenant Nelson Bronson, Captain Frederick Benteen and Captain Thomas French. Custer Battlefield Museum Collection.

BUFFALO AT BAY. Buffalo hunting could be a dangerous sport. If cornered they would charge anything in sight. In this scene taken near Fort Hays, September, 1869. General Custer may be seen just above the animal's head. Mrs. E. B. Custer collection. Custer Battlefield Museum.

BUFFALO HUNTING CAMP. Once the railroad was complete through Kansas the buffalo hunters began the extermination of the huge herds. Slaughtering them by the thousands for their hides and tongues (the tongues were a great delicacy smoked), it was but a question of time before they became extinct.

This scene near Fort Hays, Kansas was taken September, 1869. Mrs. E. B. Custer collection. Custer Battlefield Museum.

BUFFALO HUNT IN KANSAS. During September, 1869, the Seventh Cavalry was detailed to guard the construction gang of the Kansas Pacific Railroad. There was much leisure time used in buffalo hunting. Many notables and dignitaries visited Custer for the purpose of hunting with him. In the photograph above may be seen the English Lords Waterpark and Paget (marked—X). General Custer is reclining on the ground to the left; Tom Custer is sitting on the ground to the right. Mrs. E. B. Custer collection. Custer Battlefield Museum.

were to be opportunities to discuss the many cavalry actions in which they had participated against each other.

The Yellowstone Expedition left Fort Rice, D. T., in July, proceeding west to the Yellowstone River and crossing to the north side, about one hundred miles from its mouth. The country was so rough that Custer took two companies of Cavalry ahead to prepare a practicable road so there would be no delay for the main command. On the fourth of August, while several miles ahead of the command, he and the ninety men accompanying him were attacked by 300 Sioux Indians. The Indians were repulsed with subsequent heavy losses in their attempt to complete the ambush. Custer had one man and two horses wounded.

During the skirmish, two non-combatants, Veterinary Surgeon John Honsinger, Seventh Cavalry, and Mr. Baliran, a trader accompanying the Seventh, were discovered by the Indians between the command and Custer's party. Being unarmed they were overtaken and killed. Both were stripped though not scalped for Honsinger was bald and Baliran had a close haircut

CUSTER AS A HUNTER. An unusual hat for Custer since he had a preference for broad brimmed ones for the protection they offered his fair and easily burned skin. 1872. Author's collection.

BUFFALO GRAZING. The buffalo is the stupidest of animals. Should it fail to see or smell an enemy it will continue to graze while every member of its herd is shot down.

Colonel Richard I. Dodge estimated that during the years 1872-73-74, at least five million buffaloes were slaughtered for their hides. This observation was based on Kansas, Oklahoma, and a portion of Nebraska only. Photo by L. A. Huffman. Courtesy of Title Insurance and Trust Company, Los Angeles, California.

Four days later the trail of a large village was discovered. Since the trail led up the Yellowstone and was but two days old, Custer took four squadrons of cavalry and began the pursuit. Following the trail all night by moonlight, they covered thirty-three miles before resting. Remaining concealed all that day the pursuit was resumed at 6:30 a.m. and three hours later they discovered the Indians had crossed to the other side of the Yellowstone. It was obvious the Indians were moving in flight for the trail was strewn with large quantities of equipment.

The disappointed troopers bivouacked until morning when an attempt was made to cross the swift-flowing river. Various methods were tried unsuccessfully all day and at sunset they were discovered by a small party of Indians. At dawn a large party of the Indians was seen opposite the cavalry campsite and a while later parties of them were seen to cross above and below them. This the Indian ponies did quite easily for they had become accustomed to the feat. No attempt was made to stop them but the time was used in placing the troopers to best advantage under the bluffs facing the river.

As soon as the several hundred Indians on his front grew bold enough to approach, he ordered a simultaneous charge of both wings and center, and the band played "Garry Owen." The Indian resistance became feeble and finally ended in disorderly flight. The cavalry dashed forward in pursuit, the various troops vying with each other to head the advance. The Indians were driven nine miles before attempting to recross the Yellowstone. In this skirmish and in the preceding one there was a total of four men killed and three men wounded; five horses were killed, one of them being shot from under Custer. The Indians lost forty warriors though the effect of the fire on the band may have increased that number.

Custer had considerable difficulty with Colonel Stanley because of the latter's inability to stay sober while on duty, and on one occasion had to take over the command until Stanley regained his equilibrium. While intoxicated he had ordered Custer's arrest, only to apologize to him later. Custer spoke of Stanley, while sober, as being one of the most considerate, kind and agreeable officers he had ever served under.

AFTER THE BUFFALO RUN. The extinction of the buffalo meant the end of the Plains Indian's way of life for from them he was furnished with shelter, food, bedding and clothing. It was with this realization of near bankruptcy that caused him to resist so fiercely. Photo by Huffman. Courtesy of Title Insurance and Trust Company, Los Angeles, California.

THE IMPERIAL HUNTING PARTY. His Imperial Highness, the Grand Duke of Russia, was most anxious to experience a buffalo hunt. Lieutenant General P. H. Sheridan, acting as his host, made suitable arrangements for such a hunt. While in Topeka, Sheridan and those who assisted him, along with Alexis' party, had a group picture taken. Photo by J. Lee Knight, 1872. Author's collection.

Left to right, top row: Frank Thompson, Dr. Koudrine, Col. G. A. Forsyth, Count Olsonfieff, Dr. Asche, Gen. Sweitzer, Lieut. Tudeer.

Middle row: Consul Bodisco, Councillor Machin, Gen. P. H. Sheridan, Grand Duke Alexis, Admiral Possiet, Gen. G. A. Custer.

Front row: Gen. J. W. Forsyth, Lieut. Sterlegoff, Col. M. V. Sheridan.

The return trip was less eventful, the command leaving the Yellowstone on September 14th and arriving at Fort Abraham Lincoln nine days later, averaging twenty-three miles daily. The expedition had been out 95 days, made 77 camps, and traveled 935 miles.

Though Custer could have had a long leave he elected to take a short one. By the middle of October he was in Monroe visiting his parents and Libbie. He arrived just in time to attend the reunion of the Army of Tennessee held at nearby Toledo. The occasion was a happy one for the re-

ception line consisted of President Grant, General Sherman, General Sheridan, and General Custer. Each took his turn in bestowing a kiss on a pretty little girl in the line. Before long they had graduated to older girls and what had started with great dignity ended in great fun. An observant reporter kept the following score:

	Babies	Little Girls	Ladies
President Grant	19	20	38
General Sherman	34	27	28
General Sheridan	17	11	63
General Custer	13	43	67

CUSTER'S BUFFALO GUN. A 50/70 modified breech-loading Springfield rifle. Courtesy of Andy Palmer's *Great Guns.* In author's collection.

Several weeks later Autie and Libbie made preparations to return to Fort Lincoln. Leaving his aged, invalid mother was Autie's hardest trial. In the agony of parting she was carried half fainting to her bed. Libbie wrote that:

> "The general would rush out of the house, sobbing like a child, and then throw himself into the carriage beside me completely unnerved. I could only give silent comfort. . . . Such partings were the only occasions when I ever saw him lose entire control of himself, and I always looked forward to the hour of their separation with dread."

GENERAL CUSTER WITH THE GRAND DUKE ALEXIS. Custer holds a buffalo tail in his right hand. Author's collection.

KISSING GENERALS. The President's reception line in Toledo at the reunion of the Army of the Tennessee developed a novel method of getting presidential votes. What started in kissing *little* girls ended by the kissing of *big* girls. General Custer is at the left; President Grant in the center, General Sheridan and General Sherman to the right. From sketch in *Frank Leslie's Illustrated Newspaper,* November 8, 1873.

MATCH BUFFALO HUNT. When fresh meat was needed, Custer and his officers made a game of the buffalo hunt by choosing sides. At the end of a day's hunt, the side having the smallest number of dead buffalo were to provide the victors with a banquet. By A. Berghaus in *Tenting On The Plains*.

GATHERING AND COUNTING TONGUES. Since the hunt covered an area of many square miles the tongues (which were a delicacy) of the animals were presented at headquarters for a final decision. By A. Berghaus in *Tenting On The Plains*.

THE BANQUET. The occasion was one given to much story telling and kidding. By Berghaus in *Tenting On the Plains*.

GATHERING AND COUNTING THE TONGUES.

SUPPER GIVEN BY THE VANQUISHED TO THE VICTORS OF THE MATCH BUFFALO HUNT.

INDIAN BUFFALO HUNT. A primitive buffalo hunt. Before the advent of the rifle, the Indian preferred the bow and arrow. In some instances they would stampede buffalo herds over a cliff. By Schreyvogel. Mrs. E. B. Custer collection. Custer Battlefield Museum.

HUNTING ACCIDENT. While chasing a buffalo, Custer's horse "Custis Lee" veered as the buffalo turned suddenly. His cocked revolver was accidentally fired into the brain of the horse. Thrown head over heels, and still retaining his revolver, Custer leaped to his feet to prepare for a fight or a footrace. The surprised buffalo looked him in the eye for a few moments, then galloped away. By Remington in *Tenting On the Plains*.

INDIAN SCAFFOLD BURIAL. Indians frequently buried their dead by placing them on scaffolds of lodge poles, or left them in a tepee. Barry photo in Burdick collection. Courtesy of Smithsonian Institution.

INDIAN TREE BURIAL. Another method of burial was to place the body in the limbs of a tree. Barry photo in Burdick collection. Courtesy of Smithsonian Institution.

CUSTER WITH HIS SCOUTS ON THE YELLOWSTONE EXPEDITION OF 1873. General Custer holds a map at which his chief scout, Bloody Knife, is pointing. Courtesy of the Custer Battlefield Museum.

SOLDIERS' MESS. The early western army posts had few comforts. Standing while eating has certain advantages to the new cavalry trooper. Courtesy of the Custer Battlefield Museum.

BISMARCK, DAKOTA TERRITORY. In 1872 this frontier town was called "Edwinton" but was changed to "Bismarck" in 1873 near the time Custer's men arrived at Fort Lincoln across the Missouri River. Courtesy of the North Dakota Historical Society.

FORT ABRAHAM LINCOLN. The Seventh Cavalry under Custer was the first regiment to occupy this post. Goff photo, 1873. Courtesy of Custer Battlefield Museum.

OFFICERS' QUARTERS AT FORT LINCOLN. The Custer house is third from the right and was built in the fall of 1873. Wm. R. Pywell photo, 1873, courtesy of the South Dakota Historical Society.

FIRST FORT LINCOLN HOME. Built late in 1873, this home burnt to the ground that winter, the Custers losing almost everything they possessed. Mrs. E. B. Custer collection. Custer Battlefield Museum.

Capt & Mrs McDougall Charles Thompson Col Thompson
Captain Badger Col Poland Tom
ace. GH Libbie Mrs Yates Maggie Lt Varnum Mrs Moylan Lt Calhoun
Lt Hodgson Captain Yates Agnes Gen Carlin Mrs McIntosh Lt McIntosh
Captain Moylan

SEVENTH CAVALRY OFFICERS AT THE CUSTER HOME IN FORT LINCOLN. Author's Collection.

FORT LINCOLN FRIENDS. Left to right, top row: Agnes Bates, Lieut. James Calhoun, Mrs. Margaret Custer. Calhoun. Center: Mrs. G. A. Custer, General Custer, Colonel William Thompson. Front: Lieut. Fred Calhoun. 1873. Mrs. E. B. Custer collection. Custer Battlefield Museum.

CUSTER IN CIVILIAN CLOTHES. The General and Mrs. Custer saved all year for a trip east each fall. The niceties of the east were a pleasurable contrast to the hardships of frontier life. 1872. Courtesy of the Custer Battlefield Museum.

MARGARET CUSTER. The General's only sister married Lieutenant James Calhoun in 1871. He was killed at the Battle of the Little Big Horn. Author's collection.

BUFFALO BILL. The well-known hunter, scout and showman had once been a scout for Custer. Author's collection.

CUSTER AT MEMPHIS, TENNESSEE. Taken in Tennessee while traveling with the Grand Duke Alexis. Photo by Bingham and Craver. February 1872. Mrs. E. B. Custer collection. Custer Battlefield Museum.

LIEUTENANT THOMAS M. McDOUGALL. Lieutenant McDougall had charge of the pack train during the expedition to the Little Big Horn River in 1876. Courtesy of the Custer Battlefield Museum.

LIEUTENANT WINFIELD S. EDGERLY. Lieutenant Edgerly and Lieutenant Weir led the advance toward Custer's position during Custer's last battle. Author's collection.

LIEUTENANT CHARLES C. DeRUDIO. Lieutenant DeRudio was with Major Reno in his charge on the Indian village in the Little Big Horn valley. Courtesy of the Custer Battlefield Museum.

LIEUTENANT CHARLES A. VARNUM. A survivor of the Battle of the Little Big Horn. Courtesy of the Custer Battlefield Museum.

CAPTAIN THOMAS H. FRENCH. Captain French was a survivor of Custer's last battle. Courtesy of the Custer Battlefield Museum.

Chapter Thirteen

THE BLACK HILLS
EXPEDITION OF 1874

It appeared as if the Custers were to be more permanently housed at Fort Lincoln for Libbie had observed that the government had invested heavily in the Seventh Cavalry by moving it up from the South. Their house at the post had been newly built and as she approached it, for the first time observing that it was completely lighted, the regimental band broke out with "Home, Sweet Home," and then followed with Custer's favorite, "Garry Owen." The garrison was all there to welcome them.

It was a complete surprise to Libbie for the house had been completed before Autie had gone East to get her. It was not a fancy affair but larger than the houses of the other officers and was the only one plastered. Heated as it was by fireplaces, the green lumber soon warped and provided new openings to let in the subzero Dakota air. It soon took most of the time of one of the guard-house prisoners to keep the fireplaces going.

Autie had to "hold court" practically every day, for one of his duties was to settle family difficulties between the laundresses and their soldier husbands, as well as listen to the complaints of the men.

Though duty of any kind was disagreeable when the temperature went down 45 degrees below zero, there was time for pleasure, too. Balls were given alternately by each company during all the winter, and there was time for hunting. The General had a pack of forty hounds that were a constant source of delight to him. Superb horseman that he was, he was a picture to see when riding either Vic or Dandy, for both horse and man seemed like one. Wearing knee-boots, buck-skin frontier-fringed breeches and coat, a navy blue shirt with broad collar, a red necktie with the ends thrown over his shoulder, and a light broad-rimmed felt hat, he certainly could be called picturesque. He was 35 years old at the time, just under 5 feet 10 inches tall, and weighed 165 pounds. Mrs. Custer spoke of his eyes as being "clear blue and deeply set, his hair short, wavy, and golden in tint. His mustache was long and tawny in color; his complexion was florid. . . ."

One night in February a carelessly-built chimney exploded in the Custer home, causing it to take fire and burn to the ground. Though they lost almost everything they had, Tom made room for them in his house, and all the officers' families provided extra clothes to tide them over. There was little time to complain for Libbie had both sewing and social obligations, and Autie had more than 800 troopers in his charge.

The Black Hills were the cause of some concern to General Sheridan. This immense tract of

BLACK HILLS EXPEDITION WAGON TRAIN. The 110 wagons were usually arranged in four columns and flanked by protecting columns of cavalry. General Custer and his scouts led the way while a battalion of infantry covered the rear. In narrow passes and valleys the column frequently traveled in single file, as it does here in Castle Creek Valley, near Custer, South Dakota. Illingworth photo, 1874. Courtesy of the National Archives.

CAMP AT HIDDENWOOD CREEK. With over 1000 men, 1900 horses and mules, 300 beef cattle, and 110 covered wagons, this camp at Hiddenwood Creek covered a sizable area. Illingworth photo, courtesy of the National Archives.

43,000 square miles had been set aside as a reservation for the Sioux Indians through the Treaty of 1868. It had been skirted by various expeditions but none had entered it. Though various reports of daring frontiersmen told of its abundance of game, timber, water, and even evidence of gold, none had lingered and explored this mysterious area.

Bounded as it was by mountains covered with dark green fir trees that made the hills appear black and gave the area its name, it was regarded by the Sioux as a religious sanctuary or asylum and their game reserve. The story had been circulated on the

frontier that few white men had penetrated its outer rim and lived to tell of it.

Observing that the Sioux were becoming more warlike, and that since civilization bordered the Black Hills, and it could become a ready refuge for the Indians in time of war, Sheridan thought it timely to gain positive information as to its resources and topography by sending an expedition there.

On June 8, 1874, General Terry, commander of the Department of Dakota, sent orders to Custer, to prepare an expeditionary party for the purpose of reconnoitering the Black Hills region. It was to consist of ten companies of the Seventh Cavalry, two companies of infantry, and such Indian scouts as he might select, all to be ready to leave as near June 20th as possible, and to return to Fort Lincoln in 60 days. Captain William Ludlow was the engineer officer of the expedition, Professor N. H. Winchell, state geologist of Minnesota, was the geologist, George Bird Grinnell took the place of Professor Marsh of Yale College as paleontologist and zoologist, and W. H. Illingworth of St. Paul was the stereoscopic photographer. Along with the guides, interpreters, and teamsters, about 1,000 men in all, there were 110 wagons and ambulances, three Gatling guns and a 3-inch rifle.

The expedition left Fort Lincoln on July 2nd,

WAGONTRAIN. The four columns are in readiness for the day's journey. The photographer, taking his pictures in pairs for the parlor stereoscope, liked at least one-half of the picture in foreground to give it depth. When this view is placed in a stereoscope, the viewer has a feeling of observing this scene from a height. Illingworth photo courtesy of National Archives.

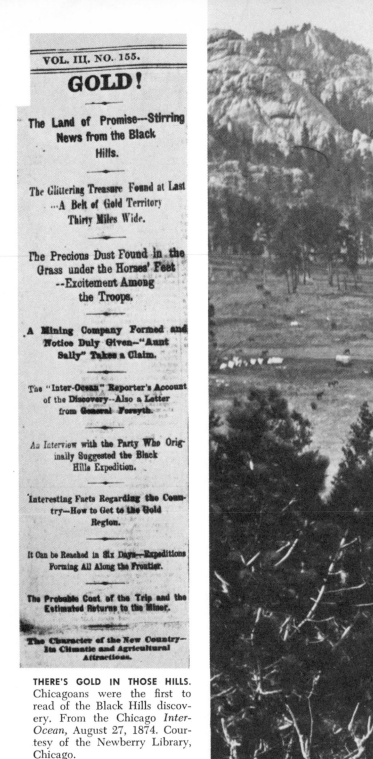

VOL. III. NO. 155.

GOLD!

The Land of Promise---Stirring News from the Black Hills.

The Glittering Treasure Found at Last ...A Belt of Gold Territory Thirty Miles Wide.

The Precious Dust Found in the Grass under the Horses' Feet --Excitement Among the Troops.

A Mining Company Formed and Notice Duly Given--"Aunt Sally" Takes a Claim.

The "Inter-Ocean" Reporter's Account of the Discovery--Also a Letter from General Forsyth.

An Interview with the Party Who Originally Suggested the Black Hills Expedition.

Interesting Facts Regarding the Country--How to Get to the Gold Region.

It Can be Reached in Six Days--Expeditions Forming All Along the Frontier.

The Probable Cost of the Trip and the Estimated Returns to the Miner.

The Character of the New Country-- Its Climatic and Agricultural Attractions.

THERE'S GOLD IN THOSE HILLS. Chicagoans were the first to read of the Black Hills discovery. From the Chicago *Inter-Ocean,* August 27, 1874. Courtesy of the Newberry Library, Chicago.

moving in a southwesterly direction. Sheridan had sent along General G. A. "Sandy" Forsyth and Lieutenant Fred Grant, the President's son. Custer also had two men who accompanied him on the 1873 Yellowstone campaign "Lonesome" Charley Reynolds and the Crow scout Bloody Knife, along with his youngest brother Boston, all three of whom were to die with him on that fateful day on the Little Big Horn two years later.

The command had little difficulty in reaching the interior of the Hills and although smoke signals were constantly around them, and a few Indians

WHERE GOLD WAS DISCOVERED. A view of Custer's Golden Valley camp showing French Creek just beyond the row of tents on the right, and with Pioneer Mountain to the left. One of Custer's miners, Horatio Ross, discovered gold here in late July of 1874. Illingworth photo courtesy of the South Dakota Historical Society.

WAGONMASTER SMITH. Captain Michael Smith, the Expedition wagonmaster, had the extremely important task of keeping all of the wagons moving. Illingworth photo courtesy of the South Dakota Historical Society.

were seen at a distance, there was no evidence of hostility. The men were constantly busied with the many duties required to obtain data for the scientific reports that Captain Ludlow would have to prepare at the termination of the trip. Everything went along smoothly for the climate was superb, the game plentiful, the scenery beautiful, and the health of the command excellent.

CASTLE CREEK VALLEY. Campsite with Castle Creek in the foreground. Illingworth photo courtesy of the South Dakota Historical Society.

THE PERMANENT CAMPSITE. Another view of Custer's permanent camp in Golden Valley near Custer, South Dakota. Pioneer Mountain in the central distance. Illingworth photo courtesy of the South Dakota Historical Society.

On July 26th Bloody Knife and a party of twenty braves discovered a village of seven lodges and twenty-seven inhabitants. The wife of the chief, One Stab, was Red Cloud's daughter. Custer approached them under a flag-of-truce and made promises of food and gifts if they would guide him. To this they agreed. Later in the afternoon One Stab and three of his men came to Custer and received presents of bacon, coffee and sugar. When accompanied back toward their camp that night three of them escaped, but One Stab was detained as a hostage and guide for several days. Just as Custer had suspected, when the camp was reached, it was discovered they had packed up and fled.

Some time was spent in a permanent camp on French Creek at what is now the outskirts of Custer City, South Dakota. Numerous side trips were made from this point and considerable additional information was obtained for the government. Custer wrote Libbie the Indians had a new name for him that he could not commit to paper but that he could tell her he had obtained the hunter's greatest prize—he had killed a grizzly.

In a report to General Terry he accounted for the mystery of the character of the interior of the Black Hills as being due not only to the obstacles one encounters at the outer base but "from the forbidding aspect of the hills as viewed at a distance, inferring that an advance toward the interior could only encounter increased obstacles." He reported an abundance of game, pasturage, pure water, timber, and ores of various kinds. In a previous report he had mentioned the presence of gold, and in his report

of August 15th he states:

"On some of the water-courses almost every panful of earth produced gold in small, but paying, quantities. . . . The miners report that they found gold among the roots of the grass. . . . It has not required an expert to find gold in the Black Hills, as even men without former experience in mining have discovered it at an expense of but little time or labor."

The expedition proceeded on its way home taking a route east of its former one. Arriving at Fort Lincoln on August 30th, the sixtieth day of the trip, the wagon train had traveled 883 miles, the total number of miles covered on reconnaissances bringing it up to 1,205.

After a short leave in New York and Monroe, the Custers returned to Fort Lincoln. Not long after the first of the new year a report came to the post that an Indian was at the Standing Rock Agency

GOLD DISCOVERER ROSS. Horatio N. Ross, one of Custer's two miners attached to the expedition, is credited with discovering gold in the Black Hills near French Creek, within Custer City, on July 30, 1874. Courtesy of the Custer Battlefield Museum.

drawing his rations, blankets and ammunition and, while doing so, was boasting of the killing of Dr. Honsinger and Mr. Baliran, two of the men Custer lost on the Yellowstone Expedition. A detachment quickly was sent out with sealed orders, since absolute secrecy was necessary, to capture an Uncpapa Indian called Rain-in-the-Face. It was a ticklish situation since there would be but 100 men and two officers in an Agency populated with 500 well-armed Indians.

PERMANENT CAMP ON FRENCH CREEK. The air was clear and fragrant, the grass and wood abundant, and the water clear and very cold. Illingworth photo courtesy of the South Dakota Historical Society.

HEART RIVER VALLEY. A typical noontime rest period. Illingworth photo courtesy of the South Dakota Historical Society.

Lieutenant Tom Custer was ordered to take five picked men, go to the trader's store, and arrest the **Indian.** It was a cold day and, since the Indians had drawn their blankets over their heads, he had to wait several hours before the one he wanted had uncovered his face sufficiently to positively identify him. Tom seized him suddenly from behind and pinned his arms while one of the soldiers grabbed his Winchester. They instantly were surrounded by about 30 menacing Indians. Tom explained through an interpreter the meaning of the arrest and that the prisoner would be given a just trial like any white man. The Indians offered two others of their tribe in exchange for Rain-in-the-Face, for he was a distinguished warrior and very brave. The march homeward was one of constant tension for they were ever expecting attack.

Custer questioned Rain-in-the-Face and succeeded in getting him to tell how he shot the old veterinary surgeon. He did not die instantly, and the Indian used a stone mallet to brain him. He then told of the younger man, Baliran, holding out his hand in peace, for neither of the murdered men had been armed, and how he shot him, first with a gun and then with arrows. The officers could hardly restrain themselves as they led him to the guardhouse.

During Rain-in-the-Face's imprisonment he was visited by a constant stream of Indians, many of importance.

It had been noted that the grain had been disappearing from some of the forage buildings at Fort Lincoln, which Custer established, having been carried over the ice to nearby Bismark. Knowing that he had no jurisdiction in that city, he was assisted by Lieutenant Carland, formerly an attorney, in gathering evidence that would stick. One day in Spring, just before the ice broke up, the entire regiment was ordered out under arms and headed for Bismark. The men and officers were as amazed as the good people of Bismark for none knew what it was all about. Custer indicated the houses and upon his insistance the doors were

RELAXATION. Though cavalrymen are known as heavy drinkers and gamblers, Custer wrote to Libbie late in August, that there had been no drunkenness or cardplaying on the trip. This party appears sober enough. Note the two stars and stripes guidons in the foreground. Illingworth photo courtesy of the South Dakota Historical Society.

OFFICERS OF THE BLACK HILLS EXPEDITION OF 1874. 1. Capt. Wm. Ludlow; 2. Capt. Geo. Yates; 3. 1st Lieut. Tom Custer; 4. 1st Lieut. Donald McIntosh; 5. 2nd Lieut. Geo. D. Wallace; 7. 1st Lt. James Calhoun; 8. 2nd Lieut. H. M. Harrington; 15. Major Geo. Forsyth; 16. Lt. Col. Geo. A. Custer; 16². a professor; 17. 1st Lieut. Tom Mc-Dougall; 18. Bloody Knife; 19. Major Jos. Tilford; 21. 2nd Lieut. Fred Grant; 22. Capt. Miles Moylan; 25. 2nd Lieut. Charles Varnum; 29. 1st Lieut. Algernon Smith; 30. Capt. Owen Hale; 33. Capt. Fred Benteen; 34. 1st Lieut. Edw. S. Godfrey; 35. 1st Lieut. Frank Gibson; 36. 2nd Lieut. Benjamin Hodgson. Balance unknown. Courtesy of the Custer Battlefield Museum.

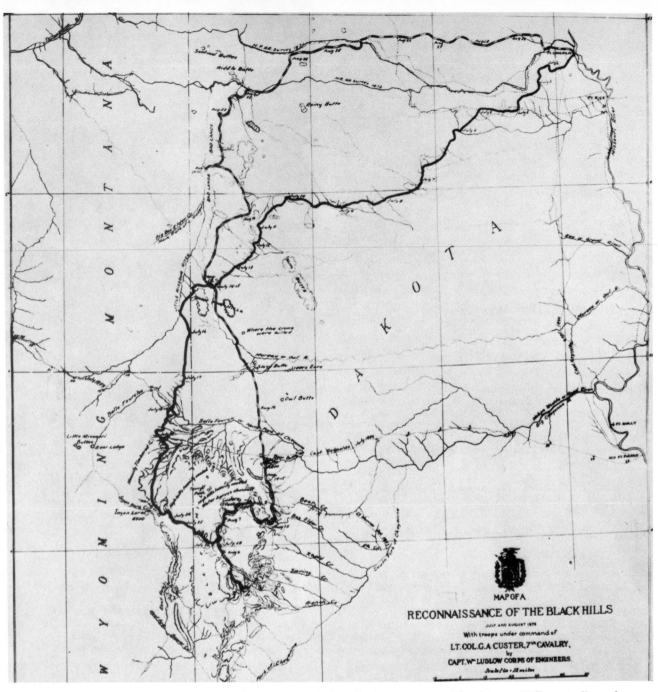

MAP OF CUSTER'S BLACK HILLS ROUTE. This is a copy of the official map prepared by Captain William Ludlow of the Corps of Engineers, showing the route of travel. Courtesy of the South Dakota Historical Society.

thrown open and in every instance stolen grain was found on the bags of which still could be seen the government brand. In the Mayor's own warehouse some bags were found. Those arrested were tried in Fargo, Dakota Territory, some time later and sentenced to the penitentiary.

A short time later two other men were caught driving wagon loads of hay off the reservation. While placed in the same cell with Rain-in-the-Face they sawed their way out of the wooden building permitting him to escape at the same time. One of the myths that evolved out of this episode

was the story that Rain-in-the-Face swore he some-day would tear out the heart of Tom Custer; and that he supposedly did that when Tom died on the Little Big Horn.

Once the newspapers of the country had printed the news of the gold find in the Black Hills, enter-prising and adventurous citizens banded together to make a rush on the Sioux domain. Arrested by the military for trespassing upon Indian lands, they quickly were released by the civil courts of the frontier. The sharp eyes of the Indians watched this encroachment upon their treaty rights with alarm for by 1875, what is now Custer, South Dakota, had grown into a small city.

Sheridan had observed the Indian unrest with alarm. It was his belief that the bands of Crazy Horse and of Sitting Bull were the nucleus of a renewed hostility. An investigation in 1875 brought out the fact that a Sioux uprising was in the making. Therefore messengers were sent to all hostile warriors telling them that they must be on their reservations by January 31, 1876. The Indians refused to comply.

The Custers spent their usual time in the East and then returned to Fort Abraham Lincoln just after New Year's day of 1876. They hardly had settled down when he received an order to be present in Washington to appear before the Committee on Expenditures in the House of Representatives. Travel weary as he was, he had to obey. General Terry reminded him that his services in the coming campaign were indispensable, and realizing the importance of the preparations necessary for the

LONESOME CHARLEY REYNOLDS. Charlie was considered one of the finest scouts in the West. Less publicized than others, he was a quiet retiring gentleman, thoroughly capable and fearless. Greatly respected by Custer, he was to die with him on the Little Big Horn. Barry photo courtesy of the Smithsonian Institution.

ELK HORNS. These elk horns found in Reynold's Valley are evidence of the abundance of game. Illingworth photo courtesy of the South Dakota Historical Society.

EXPEDITION PHOTOGRAPHER. English born William H. Illingworth was a photographer in St. Paul, Minnesota. He established himself there in 1867, becoming extremely well known for his stereographs of the Black Hills Expedition of 1874. His camera was heavy and awkward, and all of his glass plates had to be sensitized, as well as developed, on the spot. Courtesy of the South Dakota Historical Society.

For my friend J H Beard
G H Custer

expedition, tried to intercede, but with no success.

Terry had no field service against the Indians but had a brilliant Civil War record. He did not wish Crook, who had just been promoted to a brigadiership, to command the expedition; being older, and of higher rank, he was less likely to have the spirit and zeal of Custer. Since Custer had greater success in operations against the Indians than any other officer in the army, Terry desired him to take complete charge of the expedition against the hostile Sioux.

BLACK HILLS ELK. Few elk were actually seen though there was evidence of large numbers. No buffalo were seen, but there was an abundance of other game. Approximately 100 deer were killed in one day by members of the expedition, and in all, about 1000. General Custer is shown with one of the several elk bagged. Wm. R. Pywell photo, 1873, courtesy of National Archives.

FIRST GRIZZLY. Custer, in a letter from Bear Butte Creek, mentioned that he had reached the hunter's highest round of fame —he had killed a Grizzly. Left to right: scout Bloody Knife, General Custer, Private Noonan, Captain William Ludlow. Illingworth photo courtesy of the National Archives.

CUSTER'S WINTER QUARTERS. In subzero weather it required the full time of one person to keep the numerous fireplaces going. 1875. Mrs. E. B. Custer collection. Custer Battlefield Museum.

THE SECOND CUSTER HOUSE AT FORT LINCOLN. By the Spring of 1874 this house had been completed to replace the one that had burned that winter. The Wadsworth girls (Nellie and Emma) of Monroe are in the group visiting on the porch. Mrs. E. B. Custer collection. Custer Battlefield Museum.

CUSTER'S STUDY AT FORT LINCOLN. Custer was a great lover of literature spending many of the confining hours of winter pouring over the classics. Though his critics claimed Mrs. Custer wrote his *War Memoirs,* she disclaims any credit whatever. Custer did insist that she remain in the same room while he wrote them. Courtesy of the Custer Battlefield Museum.

AN EVENING ON THE POST. Any talent was certain to be exploited on the post. Outside entertainers seldom visited them: thirsty as they were for any change in their winter routine, once they discovered a cavalryman with any talent, no matter how mediocre, he was asked for repeated performances. Here Custer turns the music , 1875.

INTERIOR VIEW OF THE CUSTER HOME. A very real effort was made to provide frontier luxury. Mrs. E. B. Custer collection. Custer Battlefield Museum.

CUSTER'S BOOKS. His library consisted of classics, biographies of generals, histories, and some fiction. Author's collection.

CUSTER'S GUNS. Custer's love of guns was in their usefulness. Like most army officers he purchased and used guns other than those issued by the government, though of a calibre firing government ammunition. Author's collection.

MRS. CUSTER IN 1874. Libbie's only contact with her husband that summer was to be through letters carried by Indian scouts on ponies—what they nicknamed the "Black Hills Express."—Author's collection.

GENERAL CUSTER IN 1875. Now 35 years of age, Custer's hardships on the plains made him appear much older. The impending trip to the Black Hills country was to tax his energy considerably. Courtesy of the Custer Battlefield Museum.

CUSTER PORTRAIT. As he appeared near the autumn of 1872. Courtesy of the Custer Battlefield Museum.

CUSTER CLAN. Libbie encouraged eastern girl friends to visit her at the post. The single officers were extremely gallant and attentive making the visit a happy one for all concerned. Emma Wadsworth is shown (bottom row) with General Custer on her left and Tom Custer on her right. Mrs. Margaret Custer Calhoun is shown (top row) with her husband James on her left and Mrs. Libbie Custer on her right. Nellie Wadsworth is seated just below and to her left. The other men are unidentified. 1875. Courtesy of the J. C. Custer family.

LIBBIE'S COUSINS. Libbie's cousins from Grand Rapids, Michigan visited the Custers several times. Cousin Mary Richmond married Charles Kendall and settled in Topeka, Kansas. Left to right: Rebecca Richmond, General Custer, Mary Richmond, Libbie Custer, and Charles Kendall. Courtesy of the Custer Battlefield Museum. seum.

CHARADES AT FORT LINCOLN. Left to right: Maggie Custer, Tom Custer, Libbie Custer, Agnes Bates as "Flora McFlimsey With Nothing To Wear." Courtesy of Charles Ferguson.

AMATEUR THEATRICALS. General Custer and his sister Margaret take the role of Quaker Peace Commissioners in a Fort Lincoln *tablieux*. Miss Agnes Bates, of Monroe, sits on the floor representing a Sioux chief's daughter. 1874. Courtesy of the Custer Battlefield Museum.

AMATEUR THEATRICALS. Below, Agnes Bates and General Custer take the roles of a Sioux chief and his bride, sometime in 1874. Courtesy of the Custer Battlefield Museum.

CAMPING PARTY AT FORT LINCOLN. An outing in 1875. Left to right: *standing in back row,* Mr. Herbert Swett of Chicago, Capt. Myles W. Keogh, 7th Cavalry; General Custer, 7th Cavalry; Dr. G. E. Lord, 7th Cavalry; Lt. R. E. Thompson, 6th Infantry; *seated,* Lt. James Calhoun, 7th Cavalry; Capt. Stephen Baker, 6th infantry; Boston Custer (Gen. Custer's youngest brother); Lt. W. S. Edgerly, 7th Cavalry; Miss Watson; Mrs. James Calhoun; Mrs. Libbie Custer; Dr. H. O. Paulding, M.C., U.S.A.; Mrs. A. E. Smith; Capt. Thomas Weir, 7th Cavalry; Lt. W. W. Cooke, 7th Cavalry; Misses Wadsworth of Monroe; Lieut. Tom Custer, 7th Cavalry; Lt. A. E. Smith, 7th Cavalry. Author's collection.

A RIDING PARTY IN 1875. The officers' wives took great pleasure in these infrequent rides with their husbands. Off duty they had to remain near camp in case of Indian raids. Left to right: W. W. Cooke, Miss Emma Wadsworth, two Indian scouts, General Custer, Miss Nellie Wadsworth, Tom Custer, Libbie Custer, Mrs. Geo. Yates, Lt. W. S. Edgerly, Mrs. E. B. Custer collection. Custer Battlefield Museum.

CUSTER AND COOKE. Lieutenants W. W. Cooke and Tom Custer with their girl friends. Tom's girl is wearing his two Medals of Honor. Author's collection.

SLEIGHING IN THE DAKOTAS. In 1875 Tom Custer took Miss Wadsworth for a sleigh ride wisely placing his friend W. W. Cooke in the empty rear seat. Mrs. E. B. Custer collection. Custer Battlefield Museum.

ALONG THE MISSOURI. In the spring Tom Custer (in the front seat) and W. W. Cooke find their thoughts turning to the Wadsworth girls. 1875. Mrs. E. B. Custer collection. Custer Battlefield Museum.

Chapter Fourteen

CUSTER'S LAST BATTLE

Representative Heister Clymer, the publicity-seeking chairman of the Committee on Expenditures of the War Department, had obtained evidence that the Secretary of War, William Belknap, had become involved in the sale of post traderships. He considered it politics to play this to the greatest advantage against incumbent Republicans. By chance he had heard of Custer's complaint against exhorbitant charges the post traders were making to the members of his garrison, and he knew something of the corruption surrounding the appointment to such a lucrative position. By summoning Custer he saw an opportunity of obtaining additional information and, at the same time, take advantage of Custer's popularity.

Custer was quite disturbed at the summons for he knew that what he had to offer was only hearsay evidence. Then, too, he was working hard on his plans for the coming campaign and knew he had little time if he was to take to the field in April. But this meant little to Clymer for he had ideas of his own.

On March 29th Custer began his testimony. As he had previously indicated, he had little to offer but what had been told to him, though the Democratic press would make of him a star witness. By the time he completed his testimony some four weeks later, Clymer had drawn from him several damaging statements regarding Secretary Belknap and the President's brother, Orvil Grant. This was not to be overlooked.

President Grant was noted for his inability to forgive anyone who attacked his friends or his administration. Custer had incurred his animosity by doing both, as soon was evident. After calling on the President three different times, he wrote him a letter expressing his desire to personally remove certain unjust impressions concerning himself. President Grant refused to see him. Having tried to call on General Sherman, who was out of town, he visited the Adjutant-General and the Inspector-General and then took a train for Chicago.

The following day, May 2nd, General Sheridan received a telegram from Sherman regarding Custer in which he stated: "He was not justified in leaving without seeing the President or myself. . . . Meanwhile, let the Expedition from Fort Lincoln proceed without him." It was obviously the will of Grant. Custer was ordered to remain in Chicago.

A perplexed Custer wired General Sherman for an explanation. He reviewed his repeated attempts to see both of them, and drew attention to Sherman's statement frequently made to him as to the necessity for leaving as soon as possible. After a considerable wait and no reply he wired

Sherman again that evening requesting the privilege of being detained at Fort Lincoln where his wife was staying. He was given this permission and continued to Fort Lincoln.

On May 5th General Terry received a telegram from General Sherman repeating orders from the President that Custer would be allowed "to remain there on duty, but not to accompany the expedition supposed to be on the point of starting against the hostile Indians, under General Terry."

On May 6, Custer wired the President for permission to serve with his regiment in the field, since he could not command the expedition. He concluded by saying: "I appeal to you as a soldier to spare me the humiliation of seeing my regiment march to meet the enemy and I not to share its dangers." General Terry accompanied it with the suggestion that "Lieutenant Colonel Custer's services would be very valuable with his command."

Partisan newspapers, strictly for political reasons, made matters worse with their references to "Grant's Revenge", while the opposition on replying added additional fuel to the fire. Custer found himself in the middle of a political football game with no opportunity or desire to take either side, for he had renounced party lines years before. In effect he had become the football. Though the embittered Grant had evidenced his desire to humiliate Custer, and Sherman, as General of the Army, was forced to go along with him, Terry and Sheridan knew that Custer was the only officer capable of heading the expedition. Sheridan, back in 1869, had told Custer, "You are the only man that never failed me."

On May 8th General Terry received word from General Sherman that the President had withdrawn his objections. Custer could command his regiment and accompany the expedition.

The expedition was to be a three-pronged affair. General George Crook had ten companies of the Third Cavalry, five companies of the Second Cavalry, five companies of the Fourth and Ninth Infantry, 1,300 men in all, to form a column starting north toward the Rosebud River.

General John Gibbon moved east from Fort Ellis, Montana with four companies of the Second Cavalry and six companies of the Seventh Infantry.

General Alfred Terry left Fort Abraham Lincoln on May 17, 1876, moving west with twelve companies of the Seventh Cavalry under Custer, three companies of the Sixth and Seventeenth Infantry, three Gatling guns, and a detachment of Indian scouts, mostly Arikara. This Dakota Column

PRESIDENT U. S. GRANT. A good general, though a poor president, Grant easily hated anyone who attacked his administration. Custer was unfortunate enough to involve the President's brother in his testimony regarding the post tradership scandals. Grant never forgave him. Brady photo. Courtesy of Ansco.

reached the Yellowstone river on June 10th, and it was from this point that Major Reno and six companies of the Seventh Cavalry were sent out to scout the valleys of the Tongue and Powder Rivers. Reno swung as far west as the Rosebud River, discovering a fresh Indian trail headed for the Little Big Horn River. On the morning of June 17th General Crook's troops were attacked by a combined force of Sioux and Cheyennes on the upper Rosebud Creek, about 20 miles south and east of what is now the Custer Battlefield. After defeating Crook, the Indians advanced to the Little Big Horn, joining their tribesmen there on June 24th. Crook returned to his base, no information of the engagement reaching Terry or Gibbon until early July.

Terry's column joined that of Gibbon on June 21st at the mouth of the Rosebud. That afternoon, Terry, Custer, Gibbon, Brisbin and a few others held a conference on board the supply ship *Far West*. The general plan outlined was intended to maneuver the Indians between the two forces so that they could not run away but would be forced to fight. Gibbon was to march his men up the Big Horn River and then up the Little Big Horn

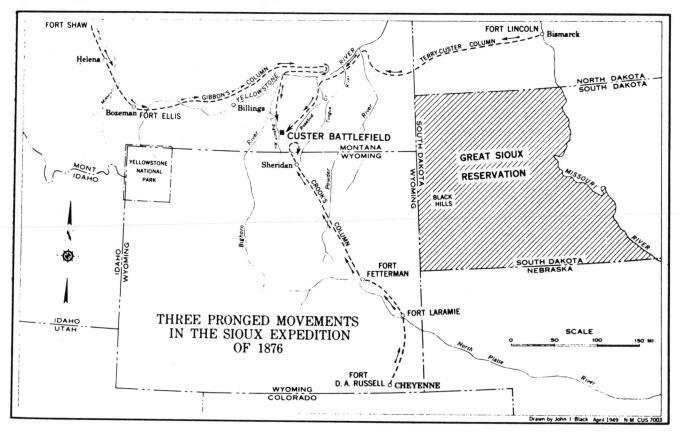

THREE PRONGED MOVEMENT.   Courtesy of the National Park Service.

river. The *Far West* was to follow as far as was practicable. Custer would take his cavalry up the Rosebud Creek, following the Indian trail discovered by Major Reno.

Custer ordered his men to carry rations for 15 days, along with 24 rounds of pistol ammunition, 100 rounds of carbine ammunition, and 12 pounds of oats. By noon on June 22nd they were packed, passing in review before Generals Terry, Gibbon and Custer, as they moved south on the Rosebud. By the evening of June 24th Custer, with more than 600 cavalrymen, 44 Ree and Crow Indian Scouts, and 20 some guides, packers, and civilians had bivouacked about 25 miles east of the Little Big Horn Valley. Near 9 p.m. the scouts advised Custer that the trail of the Indians led across the divide into the Little Big Horn Valley. He immediately informed his officers of this information, directing the march to continue so that they could get as near the divide as possible before daybreak, and there remain for an attack at dawn on the 26th. In the intense dark the column moved cautiously forward, a distance of about ten miles.

Lieutenant Charles Varnum and his scouts had reached the Crow's Nest, the high point on the divide, to await dawn. As the first sun rays penetrated the haze, the Indians were able to see the large pony herds of the Indian village 15 miles to the west. Custer was informed of the discovery, and a short time later was advised of the presence of several Sioux scouts observing his camp. Since further attempts at concealment was useless, and the chance that the Indian village would break up and scatter, he decided to strike.

At 12:07 noon of June 25th, Custer halted to divide his regiment into three battalions. Major Marcus Reno was assigned Companies A, G, and M. Captain Frederick Benteen's battalion consisted of Companies D, H, and K. And General Custer retained Companies C, E, F, I, and L. Company B under Captain McDougall was detailed to guard the pack-train. At 12:15 p.m. they moved on.

Benteen with his battalion of 125 men was ordered to scout the bluffs to the left, and to pitch into anything he could find. Further orders were given to continue on to the next valley, should he finding nothing, and then on to the next valley.

Custer and Reno continued on opposite sides of Sundance Creek for a distance of nine miles when a lone tepee was discovered containing the body of a dead warrior. As it was neared, a heavy dust cloud was seen about 5 miles away, over in the Little Big Horn Valley. It was observed that the dust was due to 40 or 50 Sioux riding between the

GENERAL ALFRED TERRY. Terry was commander of the Department of Dakota, which included Gibbon's Montana column. He left Fort Abraham Lincoln on May 17, 1876 with 925 men in his command, having placed Custer in charge of his cavalry. Courtesy of the National Archives.

GENERAL GEORGE CROOK. On June 17, 1876, just 8 days before Custer's last battle, Crook suffered a major defeat at the hands of the Sioux Indians when he attempted to force them north toward Terry and Gibbon. Courtesy of the National Archives.

GENERAL JOHN GIBBON. Leaving Fort Ellis, Montana, in April, Gibbon led his cavalry down the Yellowstone River where he was joined by a force of infantry. This column then moved east down the Yellowstone River. Courtesy of the National Archives.

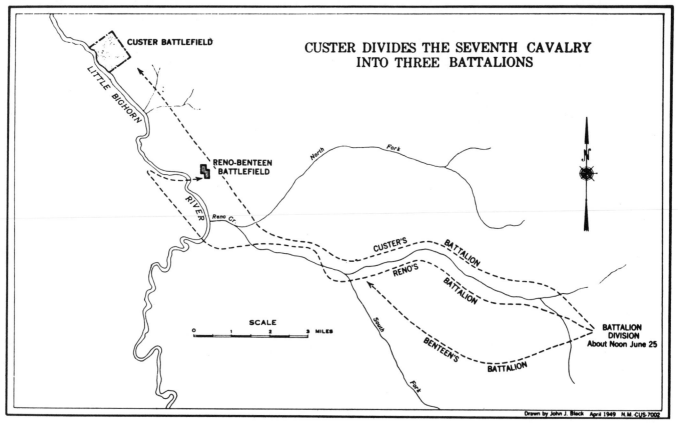

CUSTER DIVIDES HIS COMMAND.   Courtesy of the National Park Service.

troops and the river, and apparently fleeing. Lieutenant W. W. Cooke riding up to Reno said, "General Custer directs that you take as fast a gait as you deem prudent, and charge afterward, and you will be supported by the whole outfit."

Reno made the three miles to the river at a trot, crossing it at about 2:30 p.m. On the far side he reformed his lines placing A and M Companies in front, and with G Company in reserve trotted down the valley. Calling G Company into the line the battalion went into a gallop. Indians were beginning to appear out of the clouds of dust and fired at them. When Reno saw hundreds of mounted warriors appear before him, he halted his line about one quarter of a mile from the village. Dismounting his men to act as skirmishers he ordered the line to pivot to the right, placing their backs to the timber along the river.

Up to this time but one man had been shot and two had been carried into the Indian lines on the backs of their frantic and unmanageable horses. After fighting in the woods about half an hour, Reno observed that the Sioux were beginning to infiltrate the woods, and that his own ammunition was running low. An order was given to mount, and as they did so, the scout Bloody Knife was shot

through the head, his brains figuratively splashing into Reno's face. Another trooper was hit nearby.

Reno, unnerved and shaken by the sight of the large numbers of Indians opposing him, gave the order to dismount, then mount. Heading the retreat toward his former crossing he found the resistance too great and had to swerve to the left, making for the river through a pack of Sioux. On the right of the column the Indians were pumping lead into them as fast as they could. Men and horses dropped all the way. When the river was reached the cutbank had a sheer drop of six feet to the four feet of water below. Horses and men piled upon each other as the banks crumbled under them, and the frantic soldiers attempted to resist the blood-crazed Sioux.

It was a demoralized and disorganized battalion that made its weary way up to the bluffs on the opposite side overlooking the valley, for when the roll was called there were more than 40 men missing out of the original 112.

Benteen reached the top of the bluffs just as Reno's men were scaling them. He had scouted off to the left but found no Indians. Returning to follow Custer's trail he had been met by Sergeant Kanipe who had a message for the commander of

152

the pack-train to hurry up the packs. A mile further he was met by Custer's orderly trumpeter Giovanni Martini bearing Custer's message: "Benteen—Come on—Big Village—Be Quick—Bring Packs. W. W. Cooke. P.S. Bring pacs." Benteen increased his pace for now he could hear the sound of the guns in the valley, but he did not bring up the packs. Kanipe had gone on to do that.

Immediately after Benteen's arrival, heavy firing could be heard down stream. Thinking this was Custer in need of support, Captain Weir started out with his company in the direction of the firing and was soon followed by the rest of the companies. Following the ridge to the northwest for a distance of more than a mile, a high point (now Weir Point) was reached from which Indians could be seen indistinctly several miles away, firing toward the ground (the area now is known as the Custer Battlefield). Soon the Indians came back to Weir Point in such numbers that it was found advisable to return to the former location where the ground could be defended easier. Once there the heavy firing continued until dark.

The troops had used the night to feverishly prepare for the inevitable. As there were only three spades, every tool that could be improvised was used to dig shallow pits in the packed and sugary soil. Saddles, hardtack and ammunition boxes, or anything substantial, were used for barricades. While the men prepared for the coming battle the Indians could be heard wildly celebrating the victories of that day. The sky was red with their many campfires, and their weird chants kept even the stouthearted from sleeping.

With the first ray of dawn the firing began, soon growing extremely heavy. The wounded troopers were calling out for water and soon there were volunteers snaking their way down a deep ravine toward the river, their arms full of canteens and kettles. These water carriers drew a heavy fire from the Indians but that did not prevent them from obtaining what they sought. In the latter part of the afternoon the Indians began to withdraw, and soon were seen to fire the grass in the valley. It was thought that the Indians were aware of the approaching columns of Terry and Gibbon.

MAJOR MARCUS RENO. Companies A, G, and M, of the Seventh Cavalry were assigned to Reno with orders to cross the Little Big Horn River and charge the Indian camp. Courtesy of the Smithsonian Institution.

CAPTAIN FREDERICK BENTEEN. Having command of Companies D, H, and K, of the Seventh Cavalry, Benteen was ordered to scout to the left of the trail approaching the Little Big Horn River. Barry photo in Burdick collection, Smithsonian Institution.

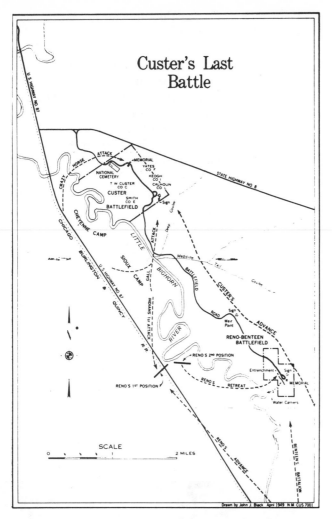

Custer's Last Battle

SCALE

0 — 1 — 2 MILES

Drawn by John J. Black April 1949 N M CUS 7001

CUSTER'S LAST BATTLE. Courtesy of the National Park Service.

The exhausted troopers stood on the hills watching the departure of the largest Indian encampment ever seen on the plains. They had not realized until now just what they had been up against. What they had thought to be 300 to 1,500 warriors, they found to be between 10,000 and 12,000 Indians, of which from 3,000 to 5,000 were warriors. The pony herd was estimated from 15,000 to 25,000, and the village was nearly four miles long, and at places, one half mile wide.

On the morning of June 27th the combined forces of Terry and Gibbon met a detachment sent forward by Reno. While jointly discussing the mysterious disappearance of Custer, Lieutenant Bradley and his scouting party returned with first-hand information. Custer and all of his 225 officers and men were dead. There were no human survivors, but a survivor there was. *Comanche*, Captain Myles Keogh's horse, was found severely wounded but, by tender care soon became his old self.

Though all of the dead troopers were stripped, and many were mutilated. Custer was one of those unmarked except for a bullet hole in his temple and another in the left breast. All of the bodies were buried on the field in what were necessarily shallow graves. In the Seventh Cavalry there had been a mortality of over 51 per cent.

Two days were required to move the wounded on mule litters. Transported down the valley to the steamer *Far West* where it was moored in the Big Horn River, the wounded were placed aboard by 2 a.m. of June 30th leaving shortly thereafter and arriving and tying up on the bank of the Yellowstone late that afternoon. At 5 p.m. of July 3rd it backed away from the bank of the Yellowstone River. Just 54 hours later this packet boat docked at Fort Abraham Lincoln, 700 miles away, a record never equaled again on the Missouri River. Captain Grant Marsh was the pilot.

Captain William McCaskey, temporary commandant at Fort Lincoln, received General Terry's communique in shocked silence early on the morning of July 6th. Requesting Lieutenant C. L. Gurly and Dr. J. V. D. Middleton to accompany him, he led the way to the rear door of the Custer quarters. Mrs. Custer's maid, Maria, was requested to bring

RELIEF MAP OF THE CUSTER BATTLEFIELD. Each line indicates the area over which each officer and his men traveled. The dark, meandering line in the foreground is the Little Big Horn River. Courtesy of the Monroe County Historical Museum.

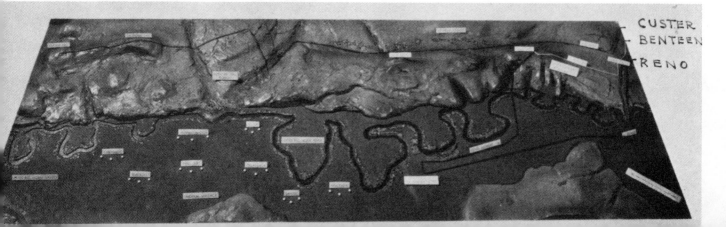

Mrs. Custer, Mrs. James Calhoun and Miss Emma Reed to the parlor.

Quickly they assembled for they had slept lightly after hearing the whistle blast of the *Far West* as she approached Bismark the evening before. Gallantly they faced what they strongly suspected, for the news was evident in the faces of the message bearers. Their grief was beyond all consolation. Finally, Mrs. Custer, though the morning was warm, drew a wrap around her. She had work to do. The other widows must be told and she would be with them in their grief.

Now what had become of Custer? Why had he not supported Reno as he had said? He had followed Reno at a slower gait but when about one-half mile from the ford had turned north and proceeded several miles at a gallop. Nearing a high point 300 feet above the valley he approached the edge in time to see Reno and his men come to a halt and dismount as skirmishers.

FIRST CUSTER BATTLEFIELD MAP. Made June 28, 1876 by Lieutenant Edward Maguire of the Corps of Engineers. Courtesy of the National Archives.

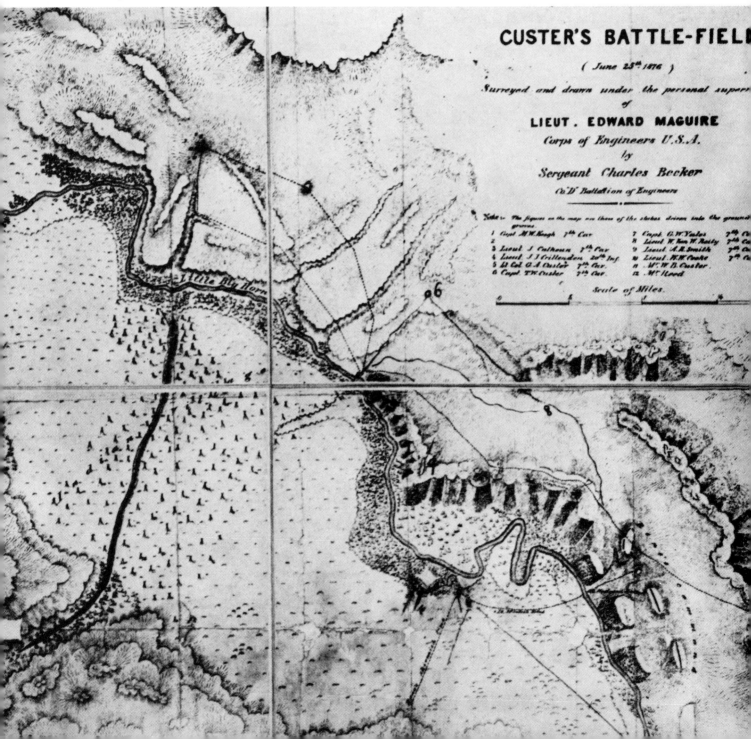

WATER CARRIERS' RAVINE. Brave troopers, who later were awarded Medals of Honor, crept down this ravine to the river's edge below under a galling Indian fire, to fill canteens of water for the wounded. Authors' photo.

For the first time he was viewing the immensity of the Indian village. Seen by Lieutenant DeRudio to wave his hat, as if in approval of Reno's halt, he rode on a ways and then sent Sergeant Kanipe with the message to the pack train to come straight across the country.

Traveling on to Weir Point more observations were made, after which he sent his orderly Martini with the order to Benteen: "Benteen, come on, big village, be quick, bring packs. P.S. Bring pacs," which was signed by his orderly W. W. Cooke. As this was the last point at which Custer and his men were seen alive by any white man, what transpired thereafter is mere conjecture and has been the source of countless arguments and articles these many years since. The Indians did not see the column for some time later, and what they did see has provided a variety of accounts.

It seems obvious that, once Custer had seen the immensity of the village, his every action indicated he was looking for a *holding position* to which he could draw Reno and Benteen, and then "hole up" until Terry and Gibbon arrived. Once he had sent

Martini with his last message, it is believed by many students that he moved rapidly down a narrow valley to Medicine Tail Coulee about two miles east of the Little Big Horn River. Moving down the coulee toward the river one can readily see the high battlefield ridge to the west. Custer apparently crossed over it with four of his troops, sending the Gray Horse troop down the coulee toward the village to worry the Indians, while he gained his objective without delay.

The Gray Horse troopers caused considerable alarm in the village before turning north and joining the battalion, but once together they proceeded to the west end of the battle ridge. There was considerable sniping and skirmishing here for about an hour or more when they noticed Reno's and Benteen's troops on Weir Point, some three miles to the southeast.

Apparently Custer could not be seen for he was at a lower elevation, while Reno's men were silhouetted against the sky. Once aware of this, Custer ordered C and E troops a mile south of the ridge to form a skirmish line to act as a beacon. They

RENO BATTLE AREA. 1. Bluffs in the foreground to which Reno retreated. 2. Little Big Horn was crossed near the center of picture. 3. The valley beyond is the area over which he advanced (left to right) and then retreated to cross the river (from right to center). Author's photo.

never were seen by Reno but were observed by a horde of Indians hidden in a deep ravine near this line. Suddenly rising out of their hiding place they were, by the suddenness of their move, able to destroy about 50 of these troopers, the balance retreating to Custer Hill. Now having lost one fourth of his battalion, and the troops he had seen on Weir Point gone, he sent troops F,I, and L toward Calhoun Hill, hoping that they would continue on and make contact with the troops on Weir Point, and return with them to this holding position. There would be few men left to hold Custer Hill, but behind the breastworks formed by the bodies of their dead horses they must have believed it could be done.

As these companies rode eastward they had gone but a few hundred yards when they were ambushed by Sioux under Crazy Horse and Cheyennes under Two Moon, all whom were hidden under cover of the wing on the north edge of the ridge. The action from this point was fast and varied. As they retreated to the east they ran into the concealed warriors under Gall. It was all over in a short period of time, and

then the warriors returned to Custer's small band.

There remained but seven troopers barricaded behind dead horses at the top of the hill, firing slowly and with deadly precision. The hundreds of Indians who surrounded them took advantage of every bit of sagebrush and pile of earth. They crept closer and closer until some were but a few yards from the men. All at once the firing from the troopers stopped, and some of the nearest Indians yelled out that all were killed. Suddenly the seven troopers jumped up and ran for the river, making the cutbanks before they were killed.

It was Custer's last battle.

THE SIOUX CELEBRATE. The Sioux knew what Reno did not know on the evening of June 25th—Custer had been wiped out. Flushed with the victory over Custer's five troops, they were preparing for another victory over Reno the following day. Fiske photo.

CUSTER HILL. The end of the ridge on which Custer and his gallant Seventh made their last stand. The unevenness of the surrounding terrain dotted with sagebrush gave the Indians excellent cover. The large granite monument indicates the mass grave of the enlisted men. The small marble slabs show the position of each fallen trooper. Author's photo.

CUSTER BATTLEFIELD MUSEUM. A view to the southwest across Custer Hill toward the Custer Museum and the Custer Battlefield National Cemetery. Author's photo.

VICTORY DANCE. On the evening of June 25th the Sioux and Cheyennes held a victory dance in the valley below Major Reno's shallow entrenchments. Frank Fiske photo.

LOW DOG. Ogallala Sioux chieftain in the Custer Battle. Barry photo. Courtesy of Custer Battlefield Museum.

JOHN GRASS. Chief of the Blackfeet that engaged Custer. Barry photo. Courtesy of Custer Battlefield Museum.

SPOTTED EAGLE. Chief of the Sans Arc Sioux who were in the battle. Huffman photo, 1874. Courtesy of Custer Battlefield Museum.

RAIN-IN-THE-FACE. The Hunkpapa Sioux chief who boasted that he had cut out the heart of Tom Custer. Barry photo. Author's collection.

GALL. This Hunkpapa Sioux chief led the main attack against Custer after having routed Reno and his men. Courtesy of the National Archives.

CRAZY HORSE. This is thought to be a picture of that great leader of the Ogallala Sioux. He played an important part in the Custer Battle. Photo by Lt. Thomas Wilhelm, 8th U.S. Infantry, 1874. Courtesy of the National Archives.

TWO MOON. Chief of the Northern Cheyennes that attacked Custer and his men. Huffman photo, 1878. Courtesy of the Custer Battlefield Museum.

SITTING BULL. Hunkpapa spiritual leader of the Sioux. He was not a warrior and did not fight in the battle. Barry photo. Author's collection.

LIEUTENANT W. W. COOKE. As the scribe for Custer's last message, Adjutant Cooke was with Custer to the end. Courtesy of Major and Mrs. E. S. Luce.

TRUMPETER JOHN MARTINI. Martini was the last surviving trooper to see General Custer alive. He carried Custer's last message to Captain Benteen, written on a scrap of paper by Lieutenant W. W. Cooke as it was dictated to him. Courtesy of the Custer Battlefield National Monument.

CUSTER'S LAST MESSAGE. Scribbled down by Custer's Adjutant for Martini to carry, it read:

Benteen
  Come on. Big Village.
  Be quick. Bring Packs.
          W. W. Cooke
  P.S. Bring Pacs.
          Courtesy of United States Military Academy.

LIEUTENANT BENJAMIN H. HODGSON. Killed during Reno's retreat at the river ford. J. F. Coonley photo. Author's collection.

HARRY ARMSTRONG REED. "Autie" Reed, General custer's nephew from Monroe, was an adventurous boy of 18. He died but a stone's throw from his three uncles. Courtesy of Custer Battlefield Museum.

CAPTAIN THOMAS W. CUSTER. Five Monroe men died at the Battle of the Little Big Horn. Tom, though mutilated almost beyond recognition, did not have his heart torn out. He was 31 years of age. J. F. Dooley photo. Mrs. E. B. Custer collection. Custer Battlefield Museum.

LIEUTENANT JAMES CALHOUN. Married to Margaret Custer, his brother married Autie Reed's sister. The position where he fell, several hundred yards east of Custer Hill, has been named Calhoun Hill. Courtesy of the J. C. Custer family.

BOSTON CUSTER. Though 25 years old, he had five years experience as a forager before he was struck down by Sioux bullets. Courtesy of the Custer Battlefield Museum.

CAPTAIN MYLES W. KEOGH. Keogh died leading Company I on the east slope of the battle ridge. E. Klauber photo. Courtesy of the Custer Battlefield Museum.

CAPTAIN GEORGE W. YATES. Though commanding Company F, he did not die with them. His body was found on Custer Hill. Courtesy of the Custer Battlefield Museum.

LIEUTENANT WILLIAM VAN W. REILY. Reily may have been wounded or killed with his company but was not found with it. Courtesy of the Custer Battlefield Museum.

LIEUTENANT JAMES E. PORTER. Several days following the battle his buckskin coat with a bullet hole in it was found in the Indian village. Courtesy of the Custer Battlefield Museum.

LIEUTENANT H. M. HARRINGTON. A favorite of Custer's, he lost his life with him. Author's collection.

LIEUTENANT ALGERNON E. SMITH. Though commanding Company E, his body was not found with its dead, but behind a dead horse on Custer Hill. Courtesy of the Custer Battlefield Museum.

LIEUTENANT JAMES G. STURGIS. Out of West Point just one year, son of the Seventh Cavalry's colonel, Sam Sturgis, he died with Custer. Courtesy of the Custer Battlefield Museum.

LIEUTENANT COLONEL G. A. CUSTER. Though taken the year of his death, Custer had his hair cut short just before his last campaign began. He was clad in buckskin and a light broad-brimmed hat on the day of his death. Courtesy of the National Archives.

CURLY. As one of Custer's Crow Indian scouts, many think he was the last to see Custer alive. The Indian scouts had no other duty than to find the enemy (the Sioux). It was the soldiers' job to do the fighting, not theirs. Custer advised them to leave once he had found the Indian village; they followed his advice. Courtesy of the Custer Battlefield Museum.

WHITE-MAN-RUNS-HIM. One of Custer's Crow scouts. The Crows were mortal enemies of the Sioux. Courtesy of the National Archives.

GOES AHEAD. A Custer scout of the Crow tribe. Mrs. E. B. Custer collection. Custer Battlefield Museum.

HAIRY MOCCASIN. One of Custer's four Crow scouts. Courtesy of the National Archives.

ARIKARA SCOUTS. *Red Star, Boy Chief* and *Red Bear* (left to right), were "Ree" scouts with Custer. Courtesy of the North Dakota Historical Society.

STRIKES TWO. One of Custer's Arikara scouts. Courtesy of the North Dakota Historical Society.

SURVIVOR. *Comanche*, Captain Myles Keogh's horse, was found wandering on the battlefield, weak from the loss of blood resulting from numerous arrow and bullet wounds. Tenderly nursed back to health he was retired from all duties at Fort Riley, Kansas until his death in 1891 at the age of 29 years. Left to right: Blacksmith Gustav Korn, Comanche, Captain Ilsley. Mrs. E. B. Custer collection. Custer Battlefield Museum.

CUSTER HILL. Looking southwest over the stakes that mark the graves of the dead on Custer Hill, one can readily see the cottonwood trees that line the Little Big Horn in the distance, and the level valley beyond where the Indians encamped. Courtesy of the National Archives.

GLORY. Sturgis was a son of Colonel Sam Sturgis, commanding officer of the Seventh Cavalry, who had been on detached duty since the organization of the regiment. Courtesy of the National Archives.

BRAVE MEN'S GRAVES. Captain B. K. Sanderson pays tribute to an old comrade. Courtesy of the National Archives.

BATTLE'S END. There were few implements to bury the dead. The ground was hard and sugary, so that burial was but a gesture. All graves were marked with a stake in which had been driven an empty shell case containing an identification slip. Courtesy of the National Archives.

LITTER FOR THE WOUNDED. The wounded were transported to the Steamer *Far West* in litters suspended between mules. Courtesy of the Library of Congress.

CAPTAIN GRANT MARSH. Pilot of the packet boat *Far West*, his boatload of wounded cavalrymen made a record (700 miles in 54 hours) on the Missouri River never equaled since. Fiske photo courtesy of Mrs. Frank Fiske.

STEAMER "FAR WEST." Substantial and fast. Courtesy of the Custer Battlefield Museum. Photo by F. J. Haynes.

SERGEANT DANIEL A. KANIPE. Kanipe carried the first message from Custer's command, ordering up the pack train. He served in Captain Tom Custer's "C" Company at the time. Circa 1876. Courtesy of the Custer Battlefield National Monument.

BLACKSMITH HENRY A. BAILEY. As a member of Captain Myles Keogh's Company "I" he was killed at the Little Big Horn. Courtesy of the Custer Battlefield National Monument.

TRUMPETER CHARLES A. WINDOLPH. Wounded at the Little Big Horn. Received the Medal of Honor for courageously holding a position on Reno Hill that assisted in procuring water for the besieged command. Courtesy of the Custer Battlefield National Monument.

SERGEANT JOHN RYAN. Served under Captain Thomas French in "M" Company. Courtesy of the Custer Battlefield National Monument.

BLACKSMITH DANIEL NEWELL. A member of "A" Company he was wounded while in Major Reno's command. Courtesy of the Dorsch Memorial Library.

SERGEANT JEREMIAH FINLEY. Shown in full dress uniform with his horse. As a member of "C" Company he was killed with his commanding officer Captain Tom Custer at the Little Big Horn. Courtesy of the Custer Battlefield National Monument.

PRIVATE EDWARD PIGFORD. 1932. Courtesy of the Custer Battlefield National Monument. Photo by Earle R. Forrest.

PRIVATE WILLIAM E. MORRIS. Serving under Captain Myles Moylan in Company "A" he was wounded at the Little Big Horn and returned to Fort Lincoln to recuperate. Courtesy of Dorsch Memorial Library.

PRIVATE WILLIAM D. SLAPER. A Medal of Honor recipient for his part in the Custer Battle, he served in "M" Company under Captain Thomas French. Courtesy of Dorsch Memorial Library.

PRIVATE JOHN BURKMAN. As General Custer's "Dog Robber" (*Striker*) he acted as a servant as well as taking care of his horses and dogs. Though a member of Lieut. Calhoun's "L" Company, just before the battle, he was assigned to the packtrain by the general. Courtesy of the Custer Battlefield National Monument.

MONROE COMMERCIAL.

VOLUME 36. MONROE, MICH., THURSDAY, JULY 13, 1876. NUMBER 28.

THE COMMERCIAL.

Published every Thursday, at No. 19 Washington Street, MONROE, MICH., by

M. D. HAMILTON & SON.

SUBSCRIPTION—$2.00 per year, free. A discount of 50 cents for advance.

Transient advertising, per square...

JOB PRINTING—Ample facilities for all kinds of Ornamental work. Prices low and satisfaction...

CITY BREVITIES.

The weather the past week. See weather report.

C. G. Johnson, Esq., left for the Centennial, day before yesterday.

The Eagle Hose Co. will give a steamboat excursion to Sandusky in the latter part of August.

A good healthy summer drink is the lager beer made by T. B. Case, of Lasalle. 'Tis cheap too. Mr. Case comes in town two or three times a week, to supply customers.

Last Saturday evening about 9 o'clock a very bright meteor lighted up the sky, moving over our city in a north-westerly direction. Its track through the sky could be seen for 20 or 30 minutes.

Sackett's show window, contains the portraits of Gen. Custer, Thomas and Custer, and Armstrong Reed, in mourning and surrounded by a profusion of American colors.

Casualties.

CUSTER FALLEN!

TRIBUTE TO HIS MEMORY!

Our City in Mourning!

PUBLIC MEETING AT THE COURT HOUSE!

BUSINESS CLOSED!

Speeches, Resolutions, &c. &c

The news which reached this city last Thursday morning, of the death of the heroic Custer and his brave comrads is confirmed in all its fulness and terrible extent. As soon as our citizens fully realized the calamity that had befallen them—that had befallen our State and our country at large, a gloom settled upon every heart, like a pall. For Custer belonged to his country. Michigan honored him and gloried in his military career: and here at Monroe, in the home of his school days and young manhood, kindred and friends have watched his career with loving pride.

BIOGRAPHICAL.

Gen. George Armstrong Custer was born at New Rumley, Harrison Co., O., Dec. 5th, 1839. In 1842 he came to Monroe to reside with his brother in law, David Reed, and attended school here several years. He always after called Monroe his home.

THE REGATTA!

The Champions of the World in Monroe!

And their Names are Sho-wae-cae-mette!

The Floral City Club Captures the Four Oared Junior Prizes!

A CLEAN SWEEP FOR MONROE!

The eighth annual regatta of the North Western Amateur Rowing Association, held in Toledo on the 4th, 5th and 6th, was by far the finest regatta ever held by the association, and equaled, if not surpassed, any regatta ever held in the East.

A Monument to Gen. Custer.

Ed. Commercial.—Believing it will meet the views of many military and civilian friends of the late Gen. Custer in Monroe and throughout the land, I would suggest that a meeting be held immediately for the purpose of taking steps to secure donations from citizens here and Gen. Custer's friends wherever they may reside, in this or other States, to erect a suitable monument on our Public Square, to him who has so greatly distinguished his own name and left so glorious an example for the young men of our common country.

I would name Col. Grosvenor, Geo. Spalding, R. F. Phinney, Harry A. Conant, John M. Bulkley and John R. Bush, to take the matter in charge and call a meeting at such time and place as they may direct.

Respectfully,
CHAS. G. JOHNSON.

MONROE MOURNS. At the time of the battle the General's mother, father, and Brother Nevin's family lived in Monroe. All were members of the Methodist Episcopal church there. Courtesy of the Monroe County Historical Society.

174

Chapter Fifteen

HERO OR FOOL

The nation was stunned when the news of the disaster struck the front pages. GENERAL CUSTER AND 261 MEN MASSACRED! SQUAWS MUTILATE AND ROB THE DEAD! NO SURVIVORS TO TELL THE STORY!

Why had it happened? Who was to blame? No correct answers could be given at so early a date, therefore, rumors grew thick and fast. Even griefstricken Monroe, claiming five among the dead, had heard many "facts" by the route of rumor. Perhaps they were augmented by the fact that they would have to wait until the next issue of the local weekly papers for a more complete coverage of the appalling event. All rumors improve in the telling, time adding much to the luster of the story.

Today many of the facts are known. Undoubtedly the principal cause of the disaster was the lack of correct information from the Indian agents as to the number of Indians peacefully residing upon their reservations. Almost a month after Custer was killed, Sheridan asked Secretary Chandler for the authority to take over the Sioux agencies so his officers could arrest, disarm, and dismount the hostile Sioux.

On July 22nd he had Chandler's assent, and by September 1st he had made a count of all Indians. It was then that he discovered that Custer had been misinformed by the Indian agents. There had been less than half of the peaceful Indians at the reservation reported to him, the balance having been issued arms, ammunition, and rations in time to enter the battle against the Seventh Cavalry. Custer had struck a village three times the size he had anticipated, from information furnished him by the supposedly reliable Indian agents.

A sense of fairness seemed to have prevailed in the Indian Department for they had issued repeating Winchester rifles and an abundant supply of ammunition to the Sioux, for the purpose of hunting buffalo. The cavalrymen were supplied with singleshot, breech-loading Springfield carbines that overheated and jammed after firing several shells, and required a knifeblade to extract the jammed shell. Little did Custer expect to find the Indians armed with anything other than some muskets, and bows and arrows.

Another factor to consider is his division of the regiment into three battalions. The one troop that was sent to guard the packtrain can be disregarded; this was a customary precautionary measure adopted in such warfare. Much has been made of his orders sending Benteen and his 110 men to the left "valley hunting," and then sending Reno and about 150 men to attack the village, while

175

TENTH ANNIVERSARY OF THE CUSTER BATTLE. Over the years this hallowed ground has become a Mecca for countless thousands. On the anniversary in 1886 just twelve people paid tribute to the brave men who fell in this last great battle of a proud race. As the years rolled around the anniversaries became a cooperative ceremony in memory of the brave dead of both sides, for each believed that his cause was just. Each June 25th thousands of people attend the ceremony in which both Indian and soldier stand side by side as taps are blown and volleys are fired over Custer Hill. Left to right: Corporal Hall, Sergeant Horn, Capt. T. M. McDougall, Mrs. Mann, Capt. F. W. Benteen, Capt. E. S. Godfrey, Mrs. Benteen, Dr. H. R. Porter, Mrs. Garity, Capt. E. S. Edgerly, Trumpeter Renwell, White Swan. Barry photo, 1886. Courtesy of the Custer Battlefield Museum.

he took his 225 men along the east side of the ridge and made no apparent attempt to support Reno as he had indicated he would. This dividing of his forces and attacking from all sides was a method he had successfully used before against this enemy that had never been known to stand up against a cavalry charge.

Previous experience had proven that the Indians became will-o-the-wisps when permitted any avenue of escape. Standing and fighting as they did

was a tremendous surprise. Whatever plan he may have had at the moment he sent Reno in, he most certainly had to change when he saw the village size, for it was then he decided on a holding position.

This brings up the point of not having proper intelligence of the situation through reconnaissance. About ten days before the battle Terry had ordered Reno out on a scout and he had discovered the trail which had led to the village. Custer apparently had

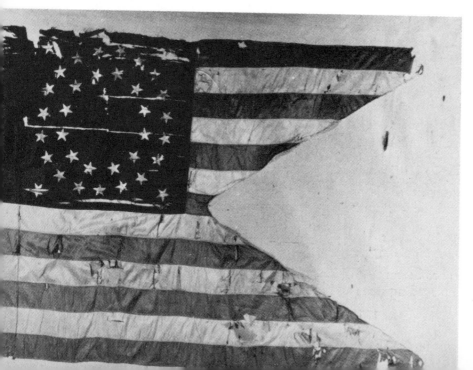

CUSTER CAVALRY GUIDON. Each cavalry troop carried one of these swallow-tailed flags. In the field they were most useful in indicating the position of a troop. Of the five that went down with Custer, the existence of two are known. This one is on display at the Custer Battlefield Museum. Courtesy of the Custer Battlefield Museum.

CUSTER MUSEUM DEDICATION. On June 25, 1952, on the 76th anniversary of the battle, the museum at the Custer Battlefield was officially dedicated. On that day General Jonathan Wainwright (center) presented a Winchester rifle, model 1866, to Major Edward S. Luce (left), superintendent of the national monument to be placed in the museum. This rifle had been used in the Custer battle but had been captured by General Wainwright's father from Two Whistle, uncle of Art Bravo (right), some years later in a skirmish with the Crow Indian tribe. K. F. Roahen photo. Courtesy of the National Park Service.

relied on the Indian agents' accounting of the number of Sioux supposedly on their reservations, for previously they had given reliable information. It was only after he had viewed the village from the bluffs for the first time that he had an idea of the immensity of the village. Reports from his scouts were so contrary to previous agency counts that he apparently refused to accept them.

Many charges and counter-charges have been made as to the supposed lack of responsibility, and even disobedience, of his junior officers. Benteen has been charged with failure to obey the "bring packs" order for, it is said, had he done so the command would have been united and had ample ammunition on Custer Hill. The unfortunate Reno was charged with cowardice in his actions in the charge toward the village and the retreat across the Little Big Horn. To Benteen can be given all the credit for restoring order to Reno's highly-disorganized battalion immediately after their retreat. So strong had grown the charges of cowardice that Reno asked for a Court of Inquiry, which was held

GENERAL CUSTER'S REMINGTON REVOLVER. Calibre .44 revolver presented by E. Remington & Sons. Courtesy of Col. Brice C. W. Custer.

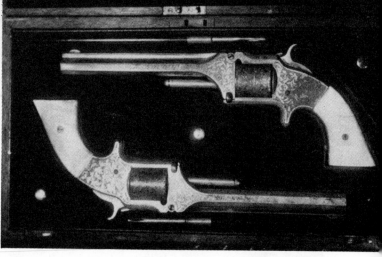

MRS. E. B. CUSTER IN 1900. On April 4, 1933 at the age of 91, the General's widow passed away in New York City. Though she was born in Monroe, Michigan, met her future husband there, was married there, and returned there after his death, she realized that with the little money she had left New York was one of the few places in that day where a woman could hope to make her own way. She devoted the remaining years of her life to the memory of her husband, demanding no part of his brilliance for herself. She was as much in love with him on the day she died as she was on the day they were married in 1864. C. W. Hill photo. Courtesy of the Monroe County Historical Society.

GENERAL CUSTER'S SMITH AND WESSON REVOLVERS. These 38 calibre guns were presented to him by Maj. Gen. J. B. Sutherland, October 1869. Courtesy of Col. Brice C. W. Custer.

in January of 1879. Reno was acquitted.

The one big criticism of Custer was that he allegedly disobeyed Terry's orders. It should be noted that the orders began as follows:

> The Brigadier General commanding directs that as soon as your regiment can be made ready for the march, you proceed up the Rosebud in pursuit of the Indians whose trail was discovered by Major Reno a few days ago. It is, of course, impossible to give you any definite instructions in regard to this movement, and were it not impossible to do so, the Department commander places too much confidence in your zeal, energy and ability to wish to impose upon you precise orders which might hamper your action when nearly in contact with the enemy.

The balance of this letter of instructions indicated Terry's views as to what should be done unless Custer saw sufficient reason for departing from them.

It was his hope that Custer's column, and the column from the north, would enclose the Indians

ONE OF CUSTER'S CIVIL WAR SWORDS. A German blade on which is engraved the legend, "No me saques sin raison; No me enbaines sin honor." (Draw me not without cause; sheathe me not without honor.) He had captured it from a Confederate officer. Courtesy of the Smithsonian Institution.

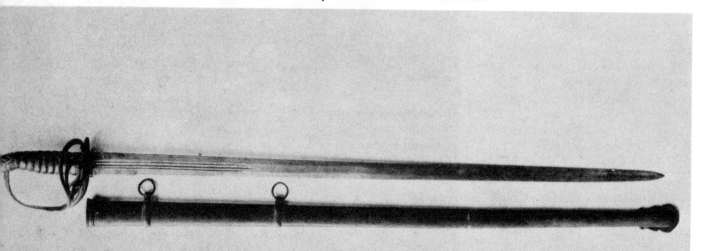

CUSTER GUNS. Some of the hunting guns used by General Custer during his moments of relaxation. Courtesy of the J. C. Custer family.

in a pincer movement. As related before, Custer elected to change both the time schedule and the suggested tactics. It is known that he was heavily-influenced in his decisions by (1) following the fresh trail Reno had discovered since it obscured the week-old trail leading to the village that would have indicated the large number of Indians that had preceded them; (2) seeing the 30 or 40 Cheyennes returning from the fight with Crook, and thinking they were running ahead to warn the village; (3) believing that the dust cloud, kicked up by herd boys rushing the pony herd into camp, was being kicked up by a fleeing village.

Custer cannot be fairly judged by the information at hand today but only by the information he had available at the time of the battle. His career had been a series of brilliant victories and achievements up to the moment this campaign began, but as on any previous occasion, each decision he made was on his own responsibility. Like any good soldier, he went into this battle to win, knowing someone had to lose. That he and his gallant men died bravely is a matter of history. Though his greatest laurels were won during the Civil War, this last battle obscured his many previous ones. Though the Indians won the battle, it was the beginning of the end for them. The nation was so aroused that there was an immediate clamor for military action against the rebelling Cheyennes and Sioux. It then became a matter of time before they were herded onto their reservation.

In 1877 the government sent a party out to the site of the Battle to exhume the body of General Custer. At Mrs. Custer's request he was buried in the cemetery at West Point. In 1933, at the age of 91, she was buried by his side.

Though Custer had many friends, there were many enemies too. Apparently the former were in the majority for today there are bronze statues of General Custer at West Point, Monroe Michigan,

BUCKSKIN COAT. While campaigning or hunting the officers of the Seventh Cavalry adopted clothing that was more comfortable or serviceable than the regulation dress uniform. In his last campaign, Custer wore a buckskin coat similar to this one he left behind. His trousers were of similar material. Courtesy of the Smithsonian Institution.

CAPTAIN CHARLES A. CUSTER. A grandson of General Custer's brother Nevin, he retired from the Army as a colonel in 1961 having served in the European theatre several times. Photo by the author in 1940.

and New Rumley, Ohio. Monroe has named streets, roads, and a school after him, and Michigan an Army camp.

A national highway reaching from Des Moines, Iowa, to Glacier National Park was named the Custer Highway: National and state parks have carried his name in the Dakotas, in addition to the Custer Battlefield in Montana, and numerous highways, markers, and monuments in that general area. Custer, South Dakota, has done much to memorialize both General Custer and the Seventh Cavalry. In the general area of Kansas, the Dakotas, and Montana, it can be said that Custer's name has been literally applied, both verbally and visually, to the theme, "Custer Camped Here." Such is the pride of association.

Over the intervening years there has been a constant stream of books, articles, paintings, and motion pictures relating to Custer and his Last Stand. Of the thousands of visitors to the Custer National Battlefield each summer many are ardent students of Custer, the Seventh Cavalry, or the battle. On a much smaller scale, the Custer Room at the Museum

of the Monroe County Historical Society has its stream of visitors with their Custer interest, for Monroe still is the home of Nevin Custer's descendants.

Many are they who claim to be of Custer blood, or a "survivor" of the battle. None can claim direct descendancy, for the general had no children. His brother, Nevin, of Monroe, was the only one to raise any children though there have been some unusual representations, like the lad who claimed the bachelor Tom Custer as his grandfather.

Of the many who have claimed to be survivors, the most recent one is a bewhiskered old fraud at Custer, South Dakota. At no time a member of the Seventh Cavalry in 1874, for he was born years after General Custer was dead, he has truly found gold in the Black Hills by selling a booklet that contains his preposterous yarn.

Today, as in Custer's day, the Seventh Cavalry is one of the top fighting units in our country. As a part of the famous First Cavalry Division, General Douglas McArthur's "First Team," it was selected by him as his escort on his official entry into Tokyo

MAJOR BRICE C. W. CUSTER. The older brother of Colonel Charles A. Custer, he too retired as a colonel (1959) having served in both the Asiatic and European theatres. His two sons are officers in the Armed Forces. Photo by the author in 1940.

THE CUSTER HOME IN 1900. The General and his brother Nevin jointly owned a 116 acre farm near Monroe on the north edge of the River Raisin. Many people of rank and position visited this house to pay their respects to the General's aging parents.

Left to right: Nevin Custer, Mrs. Nevin Custer, Annie Fisher, Armstrong Custer, Clarabel Custer. Courtesy of the J. C. Custer family.

in 1945. Five years later this same division, with the Seventh Cavalry as an active participant, was one of the first to be engaged in the bloody conflict in Korea.

Long known as *Garry Owens*, (taken from the name of the Irish tune General Custer adopted as a fighting song in 1867) the Seventh has a long and proud history. Testifying to this tremendous heritage are the following streamers that hang from the regimental standard:

Comanches	1868-1875
Montana	1873
Dakota	1874
Little Big Horn	1876-1877
Nez Perces	1877
Pine Ridge	Nov. 1890-Jan. 1891
New Guinea	Dec. 1943-Feb. 1944
Bismark Archipelago	Mar. 1944-Oct. 1944
Leyte	Oct. 1944-Jan. 1945
Luzon	Jan. 1945-Aug. 1945

Proud is the man who has served in the Seventh Cavalry, for, because of the *esprit de corps* of this superb fighting unit, it has been a match for any adversary it has ever fought.

FATHER CUSTER ON "DANDY." "Dandy" was General Custer's favorite horse. Obtained by him in 1868, he was in most of his Indian campaigns and buffalo hunts until that day in 1876. Custer chose to ride his other horse "Vic" on that day, leaving "Dandy" behind with the pack train. After Mrs. Custer returned to Monroe to mourn, all of the surviving officers of the Seventh Cavalry chipped in and shipped "Dandy" to her. She gave him to Father Custer who frequently rode him at the head of Fourth of July parades and other celebrations. C. W. Hill photo. Author's collection.

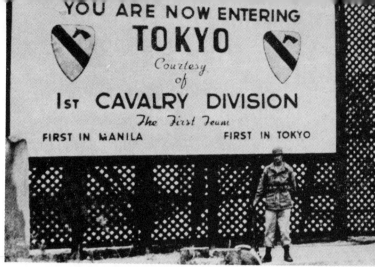

MICHIGAN ERECTED A STATUE. Erected in Monroe by the State of Michigan at a cost of $25,000 it was unveiled by Mrs. Libbie Custer on June 4, 1910. President Taft gave the principal address. Gus Beck photo courtesy of Florence Gesell.

THE FIRST TEAM. The Seventh Cavalry, a part of the First Cavalry division, had the honor of escorting General Douglas MacArthur on his official entry into the city of Tokyo. He referred to the Division as his "First Team." Courtesy of the First Cavalry Division Association.

REGIMENTAL INSIGNIA—SEVENTH CAVALRY. Frequently used by former Seventh Calvalry troopers as a lapel pin or car insignia. Colonel William (Wild Bill) Harris, now a Major General, commander of the Seventh Cavalry in the early and rough part of the Korean campaign, always displayed this insignia on the front of his jeep. Courtesy of Major E. S. Luce.

REGIMENTAL COAT OF ARMS—SEVENTH CAVALRY. This coat of arms was designed by a former commander of the Seventh Cavalry and his wife, Colonel and Mrs. Benjamin H. Dorcy. They also designed the famous shoulder patch of the First Cavalry Division. Courtesy of Major E. S. Luce.

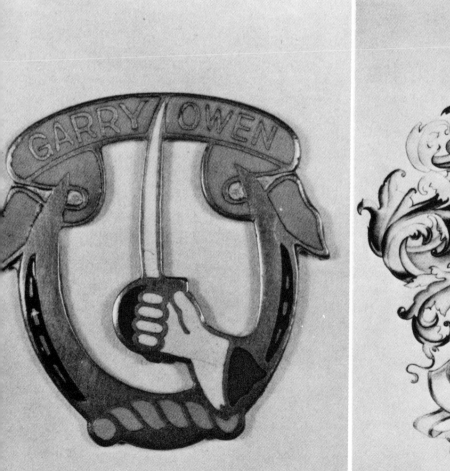

GARRY OWEN

REGIMENTAL BATTLE SONG OF SEVENTH U. S. CAVALRY

Lively

Chorus

SEVENTH CAVALRY BATTLE SONG. An Irish quick-marching or drinking song, it was adopted by the regiment as its fighting song about 1867. Its first introduction to war was at the Battle of the Washita. Popular use quite naturally brought about a popular nickname for every Seventh Cavalry trooper—*Garry Owen*—which they quite proudly accepted. Courtesy of Major E. S. Luce.

We are the pride of the Army,
And a regiment of great reknown,
Our name's on the pages of history
From sixty-six on down.
If you think we stop or falter
While into the fray we're goin',
Just watch the step, with our heads erect
When our band plays "Garry Owen."

OHIO'S MONUMENT OF GENERAL CUSTER. Erected in New Rumley by the State of Ohio in 1932 it was disapproved of by Mrs. Custer because it made her husband appear too foppish. Courtesy of the Ohio Historical and Archaelogical Society.

ACKNOWLEDGMENTS

A book of this kind is seldom the work of one person. Though credit is given below each picture I am indebted to such organizations as the:

Kansas Historical Society; Michigan Historical Society; Minnesota Historical Society; Monroe County Historical Society; Montana Historical Society; Nebraska Historical Society; North Dakota Historical Society; Ohio Historical and Archaeological Society; South Dakota Historical Society; Antioch University Library; Cleveland Public Library; Detroit Public Library; Dorsch Memorial Library (Monroe); Montana State University Library; Newberry Library (Chicago); New York City Public Library; Philadelphia Public Library; Tecumseh (Michigan) Public Library; Toledo Public Library; University of Michigan Library; Yale University Library; as well as the following individuals:

The late Forrest M. Beeson, Seventh U.S. Cavalry Association; Mr. Edward M. Beougher; Mr. Howard Berry; Miss Mary Crowther, former Librarian of Dorsch Memorial Library; Colonel Brice C. W. Custer; Colonel Charles Custer; the late Miss Margaret Custer; Miss Miriam Custer; Mrs. Colonel Gladys Dorcy; Mr. John S. DuMont; Maj. Gen. William A. Harris; Mrs. Jack Hollingsworth; Mr. Milton Kaplan, author of *Divided We Fought,* etc.; Mrs. Florence Kirtland, retired Curator of Monroe County Historical Museum; the late Dr. Charles Kuhlman, author of *Legend into History;* the late Mr. H. B. McConnell, Cadiz *Republican;* Colonel W. J. Morton, Librarian of the U.S. Military Academy; Mr. Robert Utley; Mr. Charles Verhoeven; Hugh Shick, and my secretary, Mrs. Harriet Jennette.

There is no question that I will miss others who were quite helpful. To them my sincere thanks.

I am particularly grateful to my good friend Al Dorn for casting his critical, editorial eye over this manuscript and giving me many useful suggestions for its improvement.

Above all, my debt of gratitude to the late Major Edward S. Luce and his lovely wife Evelyn S. Luce is beyond repayment. These two wonderful people who have dedicated their lives to the development of the Custer Battlefield National Monument are a tribute to the National Park Service.

BIBLIOGRAPHY

I. BOOKS

Annual Report On Indian Affairs from 1867 to 1878.

Army Register from 1861 to 1878.

BATES, CHARLES F. *Custer's Indian Battles.* Bronxville, New York, 1936.

BOURKE, JOHN G. *On The Border with Crook.* New York, Charles Scribner's Sons, 1891.

BOWERS, CLAUDE G. *The Tragic Era.* Cambridge, Mass., Houghton Mifflin Co., 1929.

BOYNTON, EDWARD C. *History of West Point.* New York, 1863.

BRADY, CYRUS T. *Indian Fights And Fighters.* Garden City, N.Y., Doubleday, Page & Co., 1904.

BRILL, C. J. *Conquest of The Southern Plains.* Oklahoma City, 1938.

BRININSTOOL, E. A. *A Trooper With Custer.* Columbus, Ohio, Hunter-Trader-Trapper Co., 1926.

BRININSTOOL, E. A. *Fighting Red Cloud's Warriors.* Columbus, Ohio, Hunter-Trader-Trapper Co., 1926.

BROWN, G. H. *Record of Service of Michigan Volunteers in The Civil War.* Kalamazoo, Michigan, Ihling Bros. & Everard, 1903,
Vol. 31—First Michigan Cavalry
Vol. 35—Fifth Michigan Cavalry
Vol. 36—Sixth Michigan Cavalry
Vol. 37—Seventh Michigan Cavalry.

BRUCE, ROBERT. *The Fighting Norths.* New York, Brooklyn Eagle Press, 1932.

BULKLEY, JOHN M. *History of Monroe County.* 2 vols., Chicago, Lewis Publishing Co., 1913.

BURT, MARY E. *The Boy General.* New York, Charles Scribner's Sons, 1901.

BYRNE, P. E. *Soldiers of The Plains.* New York, Minton, Balch & Co., 1926.

CARRINGTON, H. B. *Ab-Sa-Ra-Ka.* Philadelphia, 1879.

CATTON, BRUCE. *A Stillness At Appomattox.* Garden City, N.Y., Doubleday & Co., Inc., 1954.

CATTON, BRUCE. *Glory Road.* Garden City, N.Y., Doubleday & Co., Inc., 1952.

CATTON, BRUCE. *Mr. Lincoln's Army,* Garden City, N.Y., Doubleday & Co., Inc., 1951.

Chronological List of Actions With Indians: 1866 to 1891. Adjutant General's Office.

CONNELLEY, WILLIAM E. *Wild Bill And His Era.* New York, Press of the Pioneers, 1933.

CRAWFORD, SAMUEL J. *Kansas In The Sixties.* Chicago, A. C. McClurg & Co., 1911.

CUSTER, ELIZABETH B. *Boots And Saddles.* New York, Harper & Bros., 1885.

——. *Following The Guidon.* New York, Harper & Bros., 1890.

——. *Tenting On The Plains.* New York, Charles L. Webster & Co., 1887.

CUSTER, GEORGE A. *My Life On The Plains.* New York, Sheldon & Co., 1874.

——. *Reports On The Black Hills Expedition, August 2, 1874 to August 15, 1874.*

CUSTER, MILO. *Custer Geneology.* Bloomington, Ill., 1944.

DALY, L. H. *Alexander Cheves Haskell.* Norwood, Mass., Plimpton Press, 1934.

DAVIES, HENRY E. *General Sheridan.* New York, D. Appleton & Co., 1899.

DEBARTHE, JOE. *Life And Adventures of Frank Grouard.* St. Joseph, Mo., Combe Printing Co., 1894.

DEFOREST, J. W. *A Volunteer's Adventures.* New Haven, Conn., Yale University Press, 1946.

DELLENBAUGH, FREDERICK S. *George Armstrong Custer.* New York, The Macmillan Co., 1917.

DETROBRIAND, PHILLIPPE. *Military Life In Dakota.* St. Paul, Minn., Alvord Memorial Commission, 1951.

Dictionary of American Biography.

DODGE, T. A. *A Bird's-Eye View Of Our Civil War.* New York, Houghton, Mifflin & Co., 1883.

DONALD, DAVID. *Divided We Fought.* New York, The Macmillan Co., 1953.

DUSTIN, FRED. *The Custer Tragedy.* Ann Arbor, Mich., Edward Brothers, Inc., 1939.

FARLEY, J. P. *West Point In The Early Sixties.* Troy, N.Y., Pafraets Book Co., 1902.

FARNSWORTH, F. E. and TROWBRIDGE, L. S. *Michigan At Gettysburg.* Detroit, Winn & Hammond, 1889.

FINERTY, JOHN F. *War Path And Bivouac.* Chicago, Donohue & Co., 1890.

FOUGERA, KATHERINE G. *With Custer's Cavalry.* Caldwell, Idaho, Caxton Printers, Ltd., 1940.

GRAHAM, W. A. *The Custer Myth.* Harrisburg, Pa., Stackpole Co., 1953.

——. *The Story Of The Little Big Horn.* New York, The Century Co., 1926.

——. *Reno Court Of Inquiry.* 2 vols., Pacific Palisades, Cal., 1951.

GRANT, JESSE R. *In The Days Of My Father General Grant.* New York, Harper & Brothers Publishers, 1925.

GREEN, HORACE. *General Grant's Last Stand.* New York, Charles Scribner's Sons, 1936.

GRINNELL, GEORGE B. *The Cheyenne Indians.* 2 vols., New Haven, Conn., Yale University Press, 1923.

——. *The Fighting Cheyennes.* New York, Charles Scribner's Sons, 1915.

GUROWSKI, ADAM. *Diary From March 4, 1861 to November 12, 1862.* Boston, Lee and Shepard, 1862.

——. *Diary From November 18, 1862 to October 18, 1863.* New York, Carleton, 1864.

——. *Diary: 1863–'64–'65.* Washington, W. H. & O. Morrison, 1866.

HANCOCK, MRS. W. S. *Reminiscences of Winfield Scott Hancock.* New York, Charles L. Webster & Co., 1887.

HANSON, JOSEPH M. *The Conquest Of The Missouri.* New York, Murray Hill Books, Inc., 1946.

HARRISON, JOSEPH T. *The Story Of The Dining Fork.* Cincinnatti, C. J. Krehbiel Co., 1927.

HAZEN, W. B. *Our Barren Lands.* Cincinnatti, Robert Clarke & Co., 1875.

——. *Some Corrections of Life On The Plains.* St. Paul, Minn., Ramaley & Cunningham, 1875.

HEITMAN, F. *Historical Register And Dictionary Of The U. S. Army.* Washington, Government Printing Office, 1903.

HESSELTINE, WILLIAM B. *Ulysses S. Grant: Politician.* New York, Dodd, Mead & Co., 1935.

HUNT, FRAZIER. *Custer, The Last Of The Cavaliers.* New York, Cosmopolitan, 1928.

HUNT, FRAZIER and ROBERT. *I Fought With Custer.* New York, Charles Scribner's Sons, 1947.

Court Of Claims Of The United States; The Sioux Tribe Of Indians vs The United States. 2 vols., 1937.

JACKSON, HELEN. *A Century Of Dishonor.* Boston, Roberts Brothers, 1886.

JENNEY, W. P. *Report Of A Reconnaissance Of The Black Hills Of Dakota.* Washington, 1876.

Kansas Historical Collections. Vols. X, XI, XV, XVI, XVII.

KEIM, D. R. *Sheridan's Troopers On The Border.* Philadelphia, David McKay, 1891.

KIDD, J. H. *Personal Recollections Of A Cavalryman.* Ionia, Mich., Sentinel Printing Co., 1908.

KUHLMAN, CHARLES. *Custer And The Gall Saga.* Billings, Mont., 1940.

——. *Legend Into History; The Custery Mystery.* Harrisburg, Pa., The Stackpole Co., 1951.

LANMAN, CHARLES. *The Red Book Of Michigan.* Detroit, E. B. Smith & Co., 1871.

LONGSTREET, JAMES. *From Manassas To Appomattox.* New York, J. B. Lippincott Co., 1896.

LOUNSBERRY, CLEMENT A. *Early History of North Dakota.* Washington, Liberty Press, 1919.

LUCE, EDWARD S. *Keogh, Comanche, and Custer.* Dedham, Mass., 1939.

LUDLOW, WILLIAM. *Report Of A Reconnaissance From Carrol, Montana Territory, On The Upper Missouri To The Yellowstone National Park And Return In 1876.* Washington, Government Printing Office, 1876.

——. *Report Of A Reconnaissance Of The Black Hills Of Dakota.* Washington, 1875.

MACARTNEY, C. E. *Grant And His Generals.* New York, McBride Co., 1953.

MANYPENNY, GEORGE W. *Our Indian Wards.* Cincinnatti, Robert Clarke & Co., 1880.

MARQUIS, THOMAS B. *A Warrior Who Fought Custer.* Minneapolis, The Midwest Co., 1931.

——. *Memoirs Of A White Crow Indian.* New York, The Century Co., 1928.

McCLELLAN, GEORGE B. *McClellan's Own Story.* New York, Charles L. Webster & Co., 1887.

McCREIGHT, M. I. *Chief Flying Hawk's Tales.* New York, Alliance Press, 1936.

McLAUGHLIN, JAMES. *My Friend The Indian.* New York, Houghton Mifflin Co., 1910.

Medals Of Honor. Washington, Government Printing Office, 1897.

MEREDITH, ROY. *Mr. Lincoln's Contemporaries.* New York, Charles Scribner's Sons, 1951.

MERINGTON, MARGUERITE. *The Custer Story.* New York, The Devin-Adair Co., 1950.

MERRIL, EDWARD. *Auld Lang Syne.* n.d., n.p.

Michigan Historical Collections. Vols. 39 and 40.

MILES, NELSON A. *Personal Recollections of General Nelson A. Miles.* Chicago, The Werner Co., 1897.

——. *Serving The Republic.* New York, Harper & Brothers Publishers, 1911.

MILNER, JOE E. and FORREST, EARLE R. *California Joe.* Caldwell, Idaho, The Caxton Printers, Ltd., 1935.

MOLE, H. H. and MILLER, R. D. *A Photographic History Of General George A. Custer's Expedition To The Black Hills Of South Dakota in 1874.* Pierre, S.D., 1940.

Montana Historical Contributions, Vols. I, II, IV, IX.

MOORE, JAMES. *Kilpatrick And Our Cavalry.* New York, W. J. Widdleton, 1865.

MULFORD, AMI F. *Fighting Indians In The 7th United States Cavalry.* Corning, N.Y., 1878.

NEVINS, ALLAN. *Hamilton Fish: The Inner Story Of The Grant Administration.* New York, Dodd, Mead & Co., 1937.

NEWHALL, F. C. *With General Sheridan In Lee's Last Campaign.* Philadelphia, J. B. Lippincott & Co., 1866.

North Dakota Historical Collections. Vols. I, VI, VII.

Official Register Of Officers And Cadets Of The United States Military Academy. 1857-1873.

Ohio Archaelogical And Historical Publications. Vol. XV.

PAINE, B. H. *Pioneers, Indians And Buffaloes.* Curtis, Nebr., The Curtis Enterprise, 1935.

PARSONS, JOHN E. & DUMONT, JOHN S. *Firearms Used In The Custer Battle.* Harrisburg, Pa., The Stackpole Co., 1953.

PAXSON, FREDERIC L. *History Of The American Frontier.* New York, Houghton Mifflin Co., 1924.

PERKINS, J. R. *Trails, Rails And War.* Indianapolis, Bobbs-Merrill Co., 1929.

PRAUS, ALEXIS A. *A New Pictographic Autobiography Of Sitting Bull.* Washington, Smithsonian Institution, 1955.

PRIDE, W. F. *The History Of Fort Riley.* Fort Riley, 1926.

Rebellion Records, War of the—Otherwise known as Official Records of the Union and Confederate Armies.

REMSBURG, JOHN E. & GEORGE J. *Charley Reynolds.* Kansas City, H. M. Sender, 1931.

Report On The Condition Of The Indian Tribes. Washington, 1867.

Reports Of The General Of The Army. 1876.

Report Of The Joint Committee On Reconstruction. 1st Session, 39th Congress. Washington, 1866.

Reports Of The Secretary of War. 1867 to 1877.

RISTER, C. C. *Border Command.* Norman, Okla., University Press, 1944.

ROBERTSON, J. *Michigan In The War.* Lansing, W. S. George & Co., 1882.

RODENBAUGH, T. F. *From Everglade To Canon With The Second Dragoons.* New York, D. Van Nostrand, 1875.

ROE, CHARLES F. *Custer's Last Battle.* New York, 1927.

ROENICK, A. *Pioneer History Of Kansas.* 1933.

RONSHEIM, MILTON. *The Life Of General Custer.* Cadiz, Ohio, Cadiz Republican, 1929.

SALISBURY, ALBERT and JANE. *Here Rolled the Covered Wagons.* Seattle, Superior, 1948.

SCHAFF, MORRIS. *The Spirit of West Point.* New York, 1907.

SCHMITT, MARTIN F. *General George Crook.* Norman, Okla., University Press, 1946.

SCOTT, HUGH L. *Some Memoirs of A Soldier.* New York, The Century Co., 1928.

SEITZ, DON C. *The Dreadful Decade.* Indianapolis, The Bobbs-Merrill Co., 1926.

SHERIDAN, PHIL H. *Outline Description of the Posts In The Military Division of the Missouri.* Chicago, Jameson & Morse, 1876.

——. *Records of Engagements With Hostile Indians.* Chicago, 1882.

——. *Personal Memoirs of P. H. Sheridan.* 2 vols. New York, Charles L. Webster & Co., 1888.

SHERMAN, W. T. *Memoirs of Gen W. T. Sherman.* 2 vols. New York, Charles L. Webster & Co., 1891.

SHERWOOD, ISAAC R. *Memories of The War.* Toledo, H. J. Chittenden Co., 1923.

South Dakota Historical Collections. Vols. II, III, VI, VII, XI, XV, XVII.

SPOTTS, D. L. *Battles And Leaders Of The Civil War.* 4 vols. New York, The Century Co., 1888.

——, and BRININSTOOL, E. A. *Campaigning With Custer And The Nineteenth Kansas Volunteer Cavalry.* Los Angeles, Wetzel Publishing Co., 1928.

STANLEY, D. S. *Report Of The Yellowstone Expedition Of 1873.* Washington, Government Printing Office, 1874.

STANLEY, HENRY M. *My Early Travels And Adventures In America And Asia.* 2 vols. London, Sampson, Low, Marston & Co., 1895.

STURGIS, THOMAS. *Common Sense View Of The Sioux War.* Waltham, Mass., Sentinel Office Print, 1877.

TALLENT, ANNIE D. *The Black Hills.* St. Louis, Nixon-Jones Printing Co., 1899.

The Tepee Book. 1916 and 1926.

TREMAIN, H. E. *Last Hours Of Sheridan's Cavalry.* New York, Bonnell, Silver & Bowers, 1904.

TUCKER, W. W. *The Grand Duke Alexis In The United States.* Cambridge, Mass., Riverside Press, 1872.

VAN DE WATER, FREDERIC F. *Glory Hunter.* Indianapolis, The Bobbs-Merrill, 1934.

WAGNER, GLENDOLIN D. *Old Neutriment.* Boston, Ruth Hill, 1934.

WHEELER, H. W. *Buffalo Days.* Indianapolis, The Bobbs-Merrill Co., 1925.

WHITTAKER, FREDERICK. *A Complete Life of Gen. George A. Custer.* New York, Sheldon & Co., 1876.

WILLIAMSON, JAMES J. *Mosby's Rangers.* New York, Sturgis & Walton Co., 1909.

WING, TALCOTT E. *History of Monroe County, Michigan.* New York, Munsell and Co., 1890.

II. MANUSCRIPTS

Court Martial of General G. A. Custer. Judge Advocate General's Office, 1867.

CUSTER, G. A. *Letters and Reports Sent During 1873.*

Invoice of The Goods Received By Board Of Officers At The Death Of Baleran Aug. 4, 1873.

JACKSON, HENRY. *Itinerary Of The March Of The United States Cavalry With Section Showing Each Days March, From Fort Hays, Kansas, To The Platte River At Fort McPherson, From Fort McPherson to the Forks Of The Republican River Thence To The Platte And From There To Fort Wallace.* 1867.

Author's Collection

III. NEWSPAPERS

Bay City (Michigan) *Tribune*—1910
Billings (Montana) *Gazette*—1951, 1954
Bismarck (North Dakota) *Tribune*—1876, 1939
Bowling Green (Ohio) *Daily Sentinel-Tribune*—1949
Chicago (Illinois) *Times*—1876, 1879
Cleveland (Ohio) *Daily Leader*—1866
Cleveland (Ohio) *Herald*—1866, 1871
Cleveland (Ohio) *Plain Dealer*—1866, 1950
Detroit (Michigan) *Advertiser and Tribune*—1867
Detroit (Michigan) *Free Press*—1951
Fargo (North Dakota) *Forum*—1950, 1951
Grand Rapids (Michigan) *Daily Eagle*—1967
Great Falls (Montana) *Tribune*—1951
Hardin (Montana) *Tribune Herald*—1951
Junction City (Kansas) *Daily Union*—1867, 1868, 1953
Leavenworth (Kansas) *Daily Conservative*—1868, 1867
Lewistown (Montana) *Daily News*—1951
Monroe (Michigan) *Commercial*—1853, 1854, 1855, 1856, 1861, 1862, 1863, 1864, 1865, 1866, 1867, 1868, 1869, 1870, 1871, 1872, 1873, 1874, 1875, 1876, 1877, 1878, 1879
Monroe (Michigan) *Evening News*—1941, 1942, 1948, 1949, 1950, 1951, 1952, 1953, 1954
Monroe (Michigan) *Democrat*—1910
Monroe (Michigan) *Monitor*—1864, 1865
Monroe (Michigan) *Record-Commercial*—1910
New York (New York) *Herald*—1864, 1875, 1876
Philadelphia (Penn.) *Inquirer*—1864
Rapid City (South Dakota) *Daily Journal*—1939
Richmond (Virginia) *Times*—1890
Sandusky (Ohio) *Register*—1867
Toledo (Ohio) *Blade*—1944, 1951, 1952
Toledo (Ohio) *Commercial*—1873
Topeka (Kansas) *State Journal*—1927

IV. PERIODICALS

Army and Navy Journal. 1869-1870.

Black Hills Engineer. November 1929, January 1930, November 1931, April 1941.

BRADEN, CHARLES. *An Incidence Of The Yellowstone Expedition of 1873.* Journal of U. S. Cavalry Association, October 1904.

BRIGHAM, EARL K. *Custer's Meeting With Secretary Of War Belknap At Fort Abraham Lincoln.* North Dakota History, April 1952.

BRININSTOOL, E. A. *Derudio's Thrilling Escape.* Hunter-Trader-Trapper, March 1933.

——. *Custer Battle Water Party.* Hunter-Trader-Trapper, August 1933.

——. Col. *Varnum At The Little Big Horn.* Huner-Trader-Trapper, June 1927.

BULL, JOSEPH WHITE. *The Battle Of The Little Big Horn.* Blue Book, September 1932.

CODY, WILLIAM F. *Famous Hunting Parties Of The Plains.* The Cosmopolitan, June 1894.

DALY, HENRY W. *The War Path.* American Legion Monthly, April 1927.

DAVIS, THEODORE R. *A Summer On The Plains.* Harpers Monthly, February 1868.

DIXON, JAMES W. *Across The Plains With General Hancock.* Journal, Military Service Institution, June 1886.

DUGARD, W. T. *The True Story Of Custer's Last Stand.* Frontier Stories, Vol. 14, No. 1.

DUSTIN, FRED. *George Armstrong Custer.* Michigan History Magazine, April-June, 1946.

EASTMAN, CHARLES A. *Rain-In-The-Face.* The Outlook, Oct. 27, 1906.

FRINK, MAURICE M. *And Battles Long Ago.* Outing Magazine, October 1915.

FROST, LAWRENCE. *Courtmartial Sentences General Custer.* Great Guns, December 1952.

FRY, JAMES B. *Custer's Last Battle.* Century Magazine, January 1892.

Galaxy Magazine. March, April, May, June, September, October, November, 1876.

GARLAND, HAMLIN. *General Custer's Last Fisht As Seen By Two Moons.* McClure's, September 1898.

GIBBON, JOHN. *Last Summer's Expedition Against The Sioux And Its Great Catastrophe.* American Catholic Quarterly Review, April 1877.

——. *Hunting Sitting Bull.* American Catholic Quarterly Review, October 1877.

GODFREY, EDWARD S. *Cavalry Fire Discipline.* Journal, Military Service Institution, September 1896.

——. *Custer's Last Battle.* Century, January 1892.

——. *Some Reminiscences, Including The Washita Battle, November 27, 1868.* The Cavalry Journal, Ocober 1928.

GRAHAM, WILLIAM A. *The Lost Is Found.* Cavalry, July-August 1942.

Harper's Weekly. 1861, 1862, 1863, 1864, 1865, 1867, 1868, 1869, 1877, 1910.

HAWLEY, PAUL R. *Did Cholera Defeat Custer?* Journal, Surgery, Gynecology and Obstetrics, May 1947.

HIXON, JOHN C. *Custer's "Mysterious" Mr. Kellogg; Mark Kellogg's Diary*. North Dakota History, July 1950.

HUGHES, ROBERT P. *The Campaign Against The Sioux In 1876*. Journal, Military Service Institution, January 1896.

HUNT, FRED A. *A Purposeful Picnic*. Pacific Monthly, March 1908.

HUNT, FRAZIER. *The Romantic Soldier*. Redbook Magazine, August, September, October, 1928.

JACKER, E. *Who Is To Blame For The Little Big Horn Disaster?* American Catholic Quarterly Review, October 1876.

Kansas Historical Quarterly. Vol. XIV.

KING, CHARLES. *Custer's Last Battle*. Harpers Magazine, August 1890.

MATTISON, RAY H. *Fort Rice—North Dakota's First Missouri River Military Post*. North Dakota History, April 1953.

McCORMICK, GEORGE R. *Man Who Fought With Custer*. National Republic, March 1934.

PRICKETT, ROBERT C. *"The Malfeasance Of William Worth Belknap*. North Dakota History, January 1950 and April 1950.

REID, RUSSEL. *Fort Abraham Lincoln*. North Dakota History, October 1946.

SANDOZ, MARI. *There Were Two Sitting Bulls*. Bluebook Magazine, November 1949.

UTLEY, ROBERT M. *The Celebrated Peace Policy Of General Grant*. North Dakota History, July 1953.

VESTAL, STANLEY. *Sitting Bull And Custer's Last Stand*. Adventure, February 1, 1932.

WILSON, JAMES G. *Two Modern Knights Errant*. Cosmopolitan, July 1891.

INDEX

The name of "General George A. Custer" was omitted from single page references because of the frequency with which it occurred.